Cacti and Succulents

Other Publications:

THE SEAFARERS

THE ENCYCLOPEDIA OF COLLECTIBLES

WORLD WAR II

THE GREAT CITIES

HOME REPAIR AND IMPROVEMENT

THE WORLD'S WILD PLACES

THE TIME-LIFE LIBRARY OF BOATING

HUMAN BEHAVIOR

THE ART OF SEWING

THE OLD WEST

THE EMERGENCE OF MAN

THE AMERICAN WILDERNESS

LIFE LIBRARY OF PHOTOGRAPHY

THIS FABULOUS CENTURY

FOODS OF THE WORLD

TIME-LIFE LIBRARY OF AMERICA

TIME-LIFE LIBRARY OF ART

GREAT AGES OF MAN

LIFE SCIENCE LIBRARY

THE LIFE HISTORY OF THE UNITED STATES

TIME READING PROGRAM

LIFE NATURE LIBRARY

LIFE WORLD LIBRARY

FAMILY LIBRARY:
    HOW THINGS WORK IN YOUR HOME
    THE TIME-LIFE BOOK OF THE FAMILY CAR
    THE TIME-LIFE FAMILY LEGAL GUIDE
    THE TIME-LIFE BOOK OF FAMILY FINANCE

Cacti and Succulents

by
PHILIP PERL
and
the Editors of TIME-LIFE BOOKS

Photographs by
Enrico Ferorelli

TIME-LIFE BOOKS, ALEXANDRIA, VIRGINIA

Time-Life Books Inc.
is a wholly owned subsidiary of
TIME INCORPORATED

FOUNDER: Henry R. Luce 1898-1967

Editor-in-Chief: Hedley Donovan
Chairman of the Board: Andrew Heiskell
President: James R. Shepley
Vice Chairman: Roy E. Larsen
Corporate Editors: Ralph Graves, Henry Anatole Grunwald

TIME-LIFE BOOKS INC.

MANAGING EDITOR: Jerry Korn
Executive Editor: David Maness
Assistant Managing Editors: Dale M. Brown, Martin Mann,
John Paul Porter
Art Director: Tom Suzuki
Chief of Research: David L. Harrison
Director of Photography: Robert G. Mason
Planning Director: Thomas Flaherty (acting)
Senior Text Editor: Diana Hirsh
Assistant Art Director: Arnold C. Holeywell
Assistant Chief of Research: Carolyn L. Sackett

CHAIRMAN: Joan D. Manley
President: John D. McSweeney
Executive Vice Presidents: Carl G. Jaeger (U.S. and
Canada), David J. Walsh (International)
Vice President and Secretary: Paul R. Stewart
Treasurer and General Manager: John Steven Maxwell
Business Manager: Peter G. Barnes
Sales Director: John L. Canova
Public Relations Director: Nicholas Benton
Personnel Director: Beatrice T. Dobie
Production Director: Herbert Sorkin
Consumer Affairs Director: Carol Flaumenhaft

THE TIME-LIFE ENCYCLOPEDIA OF GARDENING

EDITORIAL STAFF FOR CACTI AND SUCCULENTS:
EDITOR: Robert M. Jones
Assistant Editor: Sarah Bennett Brash
Text Editors: Margaret Fogarty, Bob Menaker
Picture Editor: Neil Kagan
Designer: Albert Sherman
Staff Writers: Dalton Delan, Susan Perry, Reiko Uyeshima
Researchers: Diane Bohrer, Marilyn Murphy,
Heather Mason Sandifer, Betty Hughes Weatherley
Art Assistant: Edwina C. Smith
Editorial Assistant: Maria Zacharias

EDITORIAL PRODUCTION
Production Editor: Douglas B. Graham
Operations Manager: Gennaro C. Esposito
Assistant Production Editor: Feliciano Madrid
Quality Control: Robert L. Young (director), James J. Cox
(assistant), Michael G. Wight (associate)
Art Coordinator: Anne B. Landry
Copy Staff: Susan B. Galloway (chief), Tonna Gibert,
Elizabeth Graham, Lynn D. Green, Florence Keith,
Celia Beattie
Picture Department: Dolores A. Littles, Barbara S. Simon

CORRESPONDENTS: Elisabeth Kraemer (Bonn); Margot
Hapgood, Dorothy Bacon (London); Susan Jonas, Lucy T.
Voulgaris (New York); Maria Vincenza Aloisi, Josephine du
Brusle (Paris); Ann Natanson (Rome). Valuable assistance
was also provided by Carolyn T. Chubet, Miriam Hsia (New
York); Beth Cocanougher (Scottsdale, Ariz.). The editors
are indebted to Jane Opper, Maggie Oster, Karen Solit and
Lyn Stallworth, writers, for their help with this book.

THE AUTHOR: Philip Perl is author of *Ferns* in the Time-Life Encyclopedia of Gardening. He was on the staff of *The New Yorker* for 20 years and has worked with plants as a garden designer and interior landscaper. Mr. Perl raises succulents on his blueberry farm in New Jersey.

CONSULTANTS: James Underwood Crockett, author of 13 of the volumes in the Encyclopedia, co-author of two additional volumes and consultant on other books in the series, has been a lover of the earth and its good things since his boyhood on a Massachusetts fruit farm. He was graduated from the Stockbridge School of Agriculture at the University of Massachusetts and has worked ever since in horticulture. A perennial contributor to leading gardening magazines, he also writes a monthly bulletin, "Flowery Talks," that is widely distributed through retail florists. His television program, *Crockett's Victory Garden,* shown all over the United States, has won millions of converts to the Crockett approach to growing things. Dr. Gerald Barad of Flemington, N. J., is the co-founder and first president of the New York Cactus and Succulent Society. Dr. Bruce W. McAlpin is Horticultural Specialist for the tropical plant and fern collections at the New York Botanical Garden. Dr. Donald J. Pinkava is Professor of Botany in the Department of Botany and Microbiology, Arizona State University, Tempe. Father Peter Weigand, Order of Saint Benedict, is a botanist at St. Anselm's Abbey School, Washington, D.C.

THE COVER: Its full-bodied branches covered by a network of bristling spines, an eight-year-old *Trichocereus shaferi* grows upward in a tight formation. One of many hardy cacti, this small plant—about a foot tall—can be grown indoors or out and will withstand temperatures ranging from below freezing to more than $100°$.

First printing.
Published simultaneously in Canada.
Library of Congress catalogue card number 78-58300.
School and library distribution by Silver Burdett Company,
Morristown, New Jersey.

CONTENTS

Bizarre plants with a gift for survival 1

If horticulturists were to try to develop a group of plants perfectly suited to the life style of the 20th Century, they could do no better than nature has done over millions of years in coming up with the cactus and its fellow succulents. Though it is not quite correct to say that these plants thrive on neglect, they do require far less care than most other plants—a characteristic to be admired in today's hurried world where few people can devote as much time as they would like to gardening maintenance.

Furthermore, cacti and succulents often are among the few plants that thrive in today's centrally cooled and heated homes, many of which seem as dry as the Gobi Desert. Not all cacti are desert dwellers, however, though it is true that the greatest variety of sizes and shapes is found in desert species; some are at home in the trees of a tropical rain forest or on a sandy ocean beach, while others are hardy enough to withstand frost. Among other succulents, at least two, *Sedum rosea* and *Montia lamprosperma,* manage to survive north of the Arctic Circle. Though cacti do not occur naturally to any great extent in the cooler regions of the country, many different species can be cultivated in those areas if rapid drainage is provided; it is the combination of wet soil and low temperatures that often kills them.

Cacti and succulents are able to thrive in a variety of environments because their spines and tough skins make them highly resistant to pests and predators and because their stems, leaves or roots can hold large amounts of water over long periods of time. All members of the cactus family are succulents (from the Latin word *succulentus* for juice or sap) but most succulents are not cacti. Succulents, defined by this moisture-storing ability, come from many botanical families. The agave, for example, is a member of the amaryllis clan, and the medicinal aloe, popular as a natural unguent for the treatment of burns, is a member of the lily family.

A blue-green sea of unfolding echeverias creates a pastel arrangement worthy of an Impressionist master. Resembling flowers more than foliage, these succulents are most colorful in bright sunlight.

Another succulent, the columnar euphorbia, resembles the cereus cactus in color, size and shape. But close examination of the two plants reveals an important difference: the spines of the cactus grow from areoles, small nublike structures that dot the plant in regular patterns. Flowers and new growth also sprout from the areoles, which in some cases provide insulation and are used to identify species of cacti. The spines on the euphorbia and other succulents do not grow from areoles; they come directly from the body of the plant.

Generally, though, there is little chance of mistaking the fleshy, frequently fuzzy and often breathtakingly color-suffused leaves of most succulents for the stark angularity and swollen stems of a spine-laden cactus. Despite the fact that the cactus requires little water or attention, it does more than merely bring us its undemanding qualities and, like some dull and pathetic relation, ask us to put up with it because of them. The cactus brings us beauty that is simultaneously spare and flamboyant. Its flower is not only more luxuriant than those of many other plant families (each blossom of the orchid cactus Honolulu Queen contains more than 800 stamens), but it appears to be even more spectacular because of the austerity of the background upon which it appears, much as does the orchid. (In the case of many otherwise homely orchids, the flower is the only reason for cultivating the plant; in the cactus, the flower represents an additional dividend.)

STARTLING SPLENDOR

The blossoms of one tropical group, the night-blooming cerei, a term covering some 30 genera, are famed for their size. Those of the queen-of-the-night, for example, are a foot long and 8 inches wide. Despite their size, cactus flowers are often short-lived (one glorious night in the case of the queen-of-the-night) and sometimes unbearably fragrant (the same queen-of-the-night will, during her fleeting reign, release a vanilla fragrance that will make your home smell like a confectionery store).

Not all cactus flowers are as short-lived as the flashy nocturnal cerei. Most will live as long as a week, and some of them will last considerably longer. The peanut cactus, for example, whose inch-long segments appear to be flopping lazily over each other in the pot, produces vivid red flowers in the spring and keeps them in bloom for as long as a month.

Though their beauty and ease of culture entitle them to un-qualified admiration, cacti possess another sterling attribute: their remarkable ability to adapt to conditions that once threatened to take them the way of the dodo bird. Consider the problems facing the cactus some 40 million years ago. At that time deserts as we know them today were born as a result of the upward thrust of mountain ranges and equally drastic changes in wind currents. The newly risen mountains trapped moisture-laden clouds, resulting in the formation of arid regions in areas that once had received bountiful rainfall. Trapped in this violently changing environment, the wily cactus forerunners responded by changing the conventional plant appurtenances of leaves into spines, which, with less surface area, lost less moisture through transpiration. Gradually, cacti transferred their food-processing functions to expanded stems in which they could store large quantities of water. Although cacti are relative newcomers on the evolutionary scale, they have gone further than any other plant in adapting to an environment that is harsh and low in soil nutrients.

Some idea of what cacti must have looked like before they evolved into their present form can be gained by studying the Pereskieae, one of the three tribes (Opuntieae and Cereeae are the other two) into which the cactus family is divided, rather as the ancient Romans were divided into Latins, Etruscans and Sabines. The pereskia, typical of its tribe, bears leaves, but next to the leaves on the stems are groups of spines. Pereskias, like many other plants, grow in both evergreen and deciduous varieties. Their most popular use is as a vigorous understock in the grafting of the various "holiday" cacti, such as the Christmas and Easter species. And in the Southwest they are used frequently as garden shrubs—and sometimes in boundary hedges.

The fruits of the Barbados-gooseberry pereskia are esteemed as a delicacy throughout the West Indies. Also known as the lemon vine, the plant makes a handsome hanging basket in temperate-zone homes. With its glossy, red-tinged leaves, it rather resembles the almost indestructible and therefore widely admired grape ivy. It requires a moist soil except in winter, and will reveal its cactaceous qualities only when forgetful fingers touch the undersurfaces of the leaves and brush against the lurking spines. Monthly use of a fertilizer with a high phosphorus content (indicated by a large middle number in the three-number formula used in describing most plant foods—15-30-15, for example) will improve your chances of getting large, lemon-scented blooms and even an eventual gooseberry. The wrinkled pereskia (so-called because its leaves are crumpled) produces bright red flowers and requires the same high-phosphorus diet. All pereskia flowers are borne on stalks, unlike those of other cacti, which grow directly on the plants. *Pereskia saccharosa* has huge purple blossoms, and looks, with its flowers floating upon a sea of shiny leaves, far more like a rhododendron than a cactus.

THE TELLTALE AREOLE

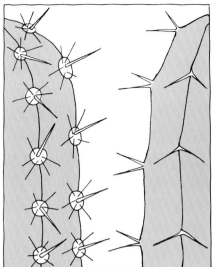

All cacti are succulents, but not all succulents are cacti. What makes a cactus a cactus is not a lack of leaves, a swollen stem or even spines. The distinguishing mark is a small, rounded cushion-like structure called an areole (left). From these areoles grow spines, hairs, branches, leaves and flowers. Other succulents, such as the euphorbia at right, may be dead ringers for cacti in all other respects, but their lack of areoles disqualifies them from being members of the Cactaceae family.

The cacti most often grown in homes are members of the opuntia tribe, the tribe most capable of causing great discomfort. Its areoles contain glochids—tufts of tiny barbed spines that will dig into the skin and produce a painful sensation long after they are, with some difficulty, removed *(page 39)*. It is prudent to keep a pair of tweezers handy when working around any cactus—especially opuntias—and many gardeners wear leather gloves, too. Even working with as gentle-appearing an opuntia as bunny ears, so named because it does indeed appear as though two, and sometimes three or four, elongated ears have popped up from the pad that supports them, can be a painfully prickly experience. The selfsame glochids and their surrounding areoles form so lovely a gold-and-brown pattern on an otherwise pale green background that they make bunny ears well worth the slight risk of sore extremities that handling them may entail.

SPINE-SHELTERED NESTS Not all creatures find the spines and glochids of the Opuntieae as intimidating as does man. The mourning dove and the wren make good use of the bristling cholla, the tree opuntia, which often grows to 35 feet or more, as strategic sites for their nests. High up in a cholla, they are well protected from the predators of the Southwest by both the spines and the elevation.

About three fourths of the 2,000 known species of cacti are members of the third tribe, the Cereeae, now also known as the Cacteae. Comfortingly for the collector, some members of this tribe bear spines but none have glochids. Unlike the flowers of the Opuntieae, which are flattish, those of the cereus tribe tend to be funnel shaped. Cereeae vary more widely from one another than do

(continued on page 16)

Beauty shaped by adversity

There are stranger shapes among the succulents than in any other group of plants. Some, like the rare Arrojadoa rhodantha (page 15), look as the mind's eye expects a cactus to look—with their prickly green columns stabbing skyward. Others, such as Lithops summitata (page 12), look more like rocks than plants—in fact, the many species of Lithops are called living stones. Both forms are the result of millions of years of selective evolution: Arrojadoa shed its leaves and adapted a columnar shape to store precious moisture in an arid environment; Lithops buried itself for the same reason.

Regardless of what brought about their present forms, though, the bizarre-looking succulents opposite and on the following pages share a surreal beauty that might have been shaped by the hand of a whimsical human artist instead of by nature.

Haworthia truncata, a windowed succulent (top) and Mammillaria elongata cristata, a densely spined crested cactus, are slow-growing, ground-hugging plants that may take years to become a few inches tall even in the best growing conditions.

The many-shaped succulents

Although many succulents, such as the glowing green *Aeonium tabulaeforme* opposite, are prized for their beauty, in or out of bloom, some have evolved forms that are admired strictly for the way they enable the plants to survive in their respective environments. *Fenestraria rhopalophylla* and *Haworthia maughanii* bear leaves that have translucent window-like tips to admit light. Both species are shown here growing aboveground, but in nature only their tips are usually visible. Another succulent, *Anacampseros papyracea*, has scales that admit light while keeping out excess heat.

LITHOPS SUMMITATA
Leaves reveal these "stones" to be plants.

ANACAMPSEROS PAPYRACEA
Scalelike leaves prevent sunburn and conserve precious moisture.

HAWORTHIA MAUGHANII
In nature, burrowing provides escape from heat.

CRASSULA PYRAMIDALIS
Tightly packed, wedgelike leaves insulate stems.

AEONIUM TABULAEFORME
Hundreds of moisture-retaining leaves make up one rosette.

EUPHORBIA COLUMNARIS
Spines line the ribs of this succulent.

EUPHORBIA OBESA CRISTATA
Convoluted ribs swell as they absorb moisture.

FENESTRARIA RHOPALOPHYLLA
This clustering baby-toes plant usually shows only leaf tips.

CEROPEGIA RUPICOLA
Flower tubes draw insects to ensure pollination.

The versatile cacti

Many gardeners new to the pleasures of cactus growing are unaware of the numerous species that lack the familiar pads, barbs or columns of the *Opuntia microdasys (left)* or the *Arrojadoa rhodantha (opposite)*. "Some people just will not believe that this is really a species of cactus," says one veteran grower in describing *Rhipsalis pilocarpa*, a tree-dwelling tropical plant. And while not even a novice would mistake a spiny *Mammillaria* or *Monvillea* for a marigold, many cacti masquerade in forms that have for centuries confounded and delighted professional botanists.

OPUNTIA MICRODASYS
Flat pads, with reduced surface area, cut moisture loss.

ASTROPHYTUM MYRIOSTIGMA
This spineless species has myriad spots for camouflage.

PERESKIA ACULEATA GODSEFFIANA
Leaves retain moisture in this primitive cactus.

MAMMILLARIA ELONGATA
Dense spines provide insulation.

14

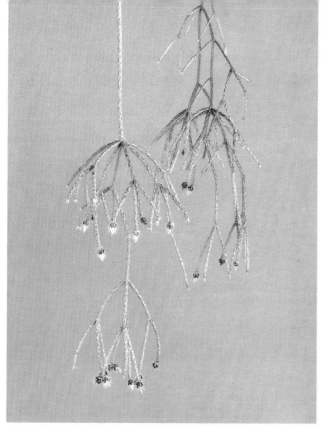

RHIPSALIS PILOCARPA
Slender stems are suspended from trees or rocky outcrops.

MAMMILLARIA INGENES
Pincushion spines are protection from enemies.

ARROJADOA RHODANTHA
Erect, slender stems may grow as tall as a man.

MONVILLEA PHATNOSPERMA CRISTATA
Contorted forms result from an abnormality in the growing tip.

members of other tribes. Roughly one fifth of them are epiphytes, or tree dwellers; these include some of the previously mentioned night bloomers. Since they are natives of tropical jungles, they require moist, lightly shaded conditions almost diametrically opposed to those required by other Cereeae, and indeed, other cacti, which are very largely desert natives.

Succulents are native to most parts of the world, but cacti are indigenous only to the Western Hemisphere—from Alaska to Chile. Within the continental United States, only Vermont, New Hampshire and Maine cannot boast a single species of native cactus, but their northern neighbor, Canada, possesses several native cacti that can tolerate freezing temperatures.

AT HOME IN THE WEST   Cacti are thought to have been contained within the Western Hemisphere by the surrounding oceans. One possible exception to the all-American provenance of the cactus is the Rhipsalis, a sub-tribe of Cereeae containing about 60 species of epiphytic cacti. The Rhipsalis species resemble the Easter cactus but their flowers are simpler and much smaller. A few species of Rhipsalis have been found in tropical regions of Africa and Madagascar, and how they got there has long mystified cactus students. In 1912, a French scientist, R. Roland-Gosselin, theorized that their seeds had been carried across the Atlantic to Africa by far-ranging birds and from there the plant spread to Europe and Southeast Asia. Indeed, the only species found so far from home bears a small, bright red berry that seems to have a magnetic attraction for birds. About 2,000 years earlier, according to one legend, Pliny the Elder was puzzled by the appearance of the prickly-pear opuntia and speculated that their seeds might have been carried by birds from some distant land. In any event, today the prickly-pear opuntia rings the Mediterranean and is as important in demarcating property boundaries in that area as fences are in American suburbs.

Indeed, the name opuntia derives not from any place in America, but from the town of Opus in Greece. The opuntia has become so thoroughly naturalized around *Mare Nostrum* that it is extensively cultivated as a food crop in Sicily. The Hebrew word for the fruit, *sabra,* has also come to mean a person born in Israel, since both are said to be tough on the outside and sweet under the skin.

Succulents other than cacti have made themselves at home all over the world, sometimes in rather surprising places. The common houseleek, or hen-and-chickens as it is popularly called, is a fixture in American rock gardens, but is native to the Swiss and Italian Alps. There are some 25 species of houseleek and their masses of colorful rosettes, which resemble flattened artichokes, can quickly take over large areas of a garden if left unchecked. The cobweb houseleek, whose leaf masses are basically bright green, is covered by a delicate web of white gossamer, but like other houseleeks it is hardy enough to be used outdoors in most parts of the United States and Canada.

Other succulents, being subject to far more lenient standards of qualification than cacti, are thought to number at least 5,000 species—and some authorities put the total at twice that. *Mesembryanthemum*, a genus of succulents found in southern Africa, contains more than 2,000 species.

Southern Africa is also the place of origin of some 200 species of aloe that produce magnificent clusters of bell-shaped flowers in reddish-gold hues. The aloe, like many other immigrants to North America, clings to at least one custom from the land of its origin: it

COPING WITH THE CLIMATE

1. *Approximately 100 million years ago, much of the western U.S. was covered with water and the land masses were steamy hothouses teeming with fantastic plants. Forerunners of cacti and other succulents had large, lush leaves.*

2. *Some 60 million years ago, mountains began to rise, leaving new land masses in their wake. The moisture-laden air blown in from the ocean was cooled as it went up the mountains; clouds formed and most of the rain fell on the western side. Lands to the east of these low-lying mountains became drier. The ancestors of today's succulents evolved thickened leaves, stems and roots to store the modest amounts of moisture that came their way.*

3. *About 40 million years ago, the high mountain ranges that still exist had formed barriers that trapped almost all Pacific rainfall on their western slopes. Plants to the east had to become even more specialized in the dry interior deserts. Thickened stems took over the job of producing and storing food and the leaves that lost too much moisture from within disappeared. Outer skins of the stems became tough and waxy so the plant could hoard moisture.*

blooms in fall and winter, when most other flowers are gone, because the cold season of the Northern Hemisphere corresponds to the aloe's original growing season in its native southern Africa.

Australia is home to only two native succulents: the Hottentot fig with its pretty 4-inch pink flowers, and the ceropegia, with curious, inflated tubular flowers, some of which are a startling chocolate color. In 1788, the Australian government, not content to leave well enough alone, began importing prickly-pear opuntias—much to its eventual regret. The cacti were to be grown not for their fruit but to nourish female cochineal bugs, which produce a natural scarlet dye when they are dried and crushed. The dye was to be used to color the famed red coats of the British colonial soldiers, but the scheme turned out to be penny-wise and pound-foolish. The opuntias, unfettered by natural enemies, ran rampant over the continent. By 1925 some 60 million previously arable acres of land, or about one third of Australia's three million square miles, were so densely covered with opuntias that they were impenetrable to farmers and probably even to cochineal-bug gatherers. The opuntias yielded to neither flame nor plow. Eventually, out of more than 100 biological controls attempted, a moth was imported from Argentina to lay its eggs on opuntia spines; in due course, the eggs hatched and the moths' larvae burrowed into the plants, causing them to collapse.

BURBANK'S BLIND ALLEY

Even so astute a horticulturist as Luther Burbank was bedazzled for a while by the prospect of riches to be gathered from the opuntia. His brother Alfred glowingly announced to the world in 1911 that the Burbank brothers had developed a spineless species of opuntia cactus that would "solve the meat problem of the future" by producing a ton of forage from a single plant in a single season, and was, in addition, hardy to 14° above zero. The brothers also had high hopes for fruit from a member of the *Cereus* genus. It was to be the size of an orange, sweeter than a strawberry and possessed of a skin that slipped off like a glove; it was "bound to become one of the most popular market fruits," they claimed. Needless to say, it did not, any more than the opuntia significantly replaced other forms of forage. The main problem with Burbank's opuntia was that it turned out to be far less drought-resistant than the indigenous species had been, and since his opuntia had no spines it made easy pickings for rodents and other pests.

Though Burbank's opuntia fodder did not rock the horticultural world as did some of his other developments (notably the Idaho potato), inhabitants of those areas where cacti grow abundantly have always known that they could depend on them for food. In Mexico, the sweet 2-inch berries of the tuna cardona opuntia are made into a

A catalogue of cactus tribes

In 1898 German botanist Karl Schumann finally established order among the bewildering array of cactus forms by dividing them by degree of evolution into three tribes: Pereskieae, Opuntieae and Cereeae (now also called Cacteae).

Members of the most primitive tribe, Pereskieae, bear broad leaves. Opuntieae, marked by the tufts of barbed bristles called glochids, survived in hot, arid regions by shifting the food-making function of leaves —present in modern forms as conical vestiges that fall off as the plant grows—to water-retaining, thickened stems. Cereeae, the most numerous and highly evolved tribe, has neither leaves—any remnants drop off in the seedling stage—nor glochids.

Pereskieae tribe

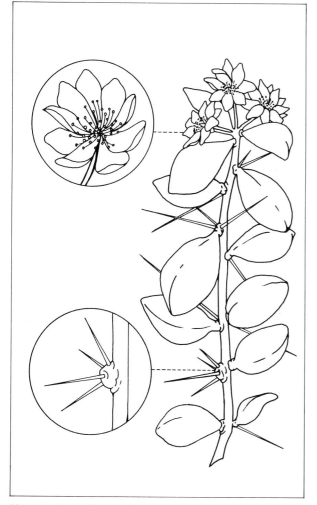

These leafy cacti are native to relatively dry tropical forests and bush country where their sprawling, generally woody stems and broad leaves are suited to the warm climate. Insets show a typically wheel-shaped blossom borne on a stalk (unlike those of most cacti) and an areole —the distinguishing feature of all cacti—from which leaves and spines grow.

Opuntieae tribe

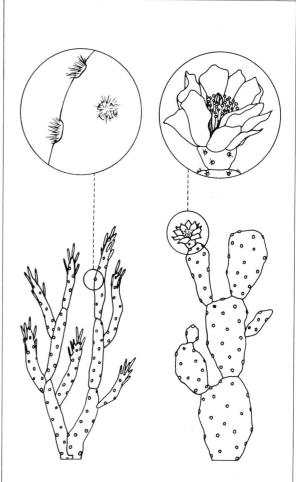

Adapting to a range of harsh, dry environments from near the Arctic Circle all the way to Chile, cacti of this tribe are marked by glochids (inset) and thickened, water-retaining stems of linked pads or a sausage-like section. Opuntieae, including chollas (left) and prickly pears (right), are the most familiar cacti. The wide open flowers (inset) have short tubes and no stalks.

Cereeae tribe

Members of the third tribe have little in common other than stalkless, funnel-shaped flowers with well-defined tubes; many also have markedly succulent stems. Because the tribe includes at least three quarters of all cacti and because its individual members are so varied, due to the vastly different environments in which they have developed, the tribe has been further divided into the eight subtribes that are illustrated here.

TORCH CACTI: CEREANAE SUBTRIBE

Cacti of the most numerous of the eight subtribes derive their name from the way they look when in bloom: like torches aflame. Upright and columnar, with ribs running vertically, members of this subtribe include some of the tallest and longest-lived cacti.

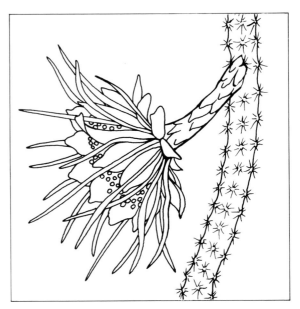

CLIMBING CACTI: HYLOCEREANAE SUBTRIBE

These are among the most graceful of cacti, with sprawling, vinelike stems that may extend eight to 15 feet and, in some cases, aerial roots that allow them to cling to rocks or trees and draw moisture from the air. Many have spectacular, fragrant flowers.

HEDGEHOG CACTI: ECHINOCEREANAE SUBTRIBE

These round cacti, generally less than a foot tall, are often covered by dense networks of spines that protect them from predators and shade their stems from the scorching sun. The plants produce outsized trumpet-shaped blossoms, which may last but a day.

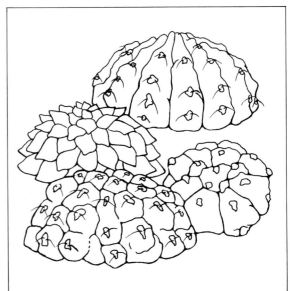

LIVING ROCK CACTI: ECHINOCACTANAE SUBTRIBE

Masters of mimicry, many of these generally midget-sized cacti blend so successfully with their surroundings that they have little need for protective spines. Flowers grow from the centers of the plants. One of the best-known is the barrel cactus.

MELON CACTI: CACTANAE SUBTRIBE

Typically melon-shaped tropical plants, the members of this subtribe may be easily distinguished from all others by the cephalium—a woolly, fezlike crown—from which tiny flowers and berries arise. The Melocactus intortus is known as Turk's-cap cactus.

PINCUSHION CACTI: CORYPHANTHANAE SUBTRIBE

These spherical, compact cacti bristle with straight or hooked spines that give the plants their nickname "pincushion." The genera Mammillaria and Coryphantha are unusual in their substitution of nipples for ribs.

TREE-DWELLING CACTI: EPIPHYLLANAE SUBTRIBE

Tropical epiphytes that use aerial roots to gather nourishment from humus in the crooks of tree branches, these cacti have wide, flat stems that resemble chains of leaves. Since the plants are safely ensconced in trees, areoles bear only tiny spines.

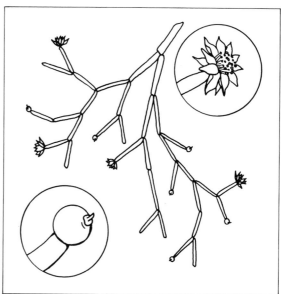

TREE-DWELLING CACTI: RHIPSALIDANAE SUBTRIBE

The second subtribe of tree-dwelling epiphytes, these cascading cacti resemble barren branches. Typically spineless and often as thin as twigs, they bear tiny white or pink flowers (inset, right) with berries (inset, left) similar to gooseberries.

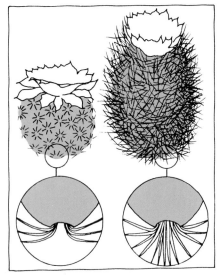

*The spines of the juvenile
Coryphanta echinus (left) differ so from
the spines of the mature plant that
scientists once listed the juvenile form
as a separate species. The neat, lacy
spines of the young plant splay out (left
diagram), allowing the flower to
open wide; the mature plant develops
long, stiff central spines (right
diagram) that keep its flowers from
fully unfolding. Many cacti alter
greatly with age, sprouting more spines
of varying color, growing hairs or
even changing shape drastically.*

preserve that holds the place accorded in England to orange marmalade. And just one giant saguaro cactus, even after a drought that has lasted as long as three years, can produce 300 fruits that look like purple hen's eggs and can be eaten fresh, preserved in their own sugar or made into wine.

Possibly even more important in economic terms than the opuntia, and certainly more so than the saguaro, is the agave, sometimes called the American aloe, a genus of 300 species of succulents that includes the misleadingly named century plant, which actually takes only 10 to 50 years to produce its enormous flower clusters on stalks up to 30 feet high. More valued for their produce than for their beauty are the henequen and sisal agaves, which yield fiber used in making rope. A pair of agaves that supply the raw material for alcoholic beverages is much appreciated by Mexicans: the pulque, which can be made into a potent wine, and the *tequilana,* whose fermented mash produces tequila, a distilled spirit of legendary strength.

The tiny dumpling cactus of Mexico and southern Texas is, despite its disarming appearance, the fabled peyote, source of the hallucinogenic drug mescaline. So potent are its hallucinatory powers that law prohibits its cultivation and possession by anyone but members of the Native American Church, which has members in several Indian tribes in the southwestern United States and requires the drug for use in its sacraments.

Though they had no way of knowing about peyote, the ancient Greeks were extracting a potent drug for mind-expanding use from aloes as long ago as the Fourth Century B.C., and King Solomon, whose interest presumably was medicinal, had raised them some 500 years earlier in his gardens at Jerusalem. The Aztec ruler Montezuma grew cacti in his gardens at Tehuantepec, which is not at all surprising, since there is a greater variety to choose from in Mexico than anywhere else in the world. What is surprising is that his gardeners sprinkled the newly planted cacti with blood taken from their own ears as a sacrifice to the gods.

Historians agree that no European had ever seen cacti, save possibly for some opuntias, before they were brought back to the continent by early missionaries. The cacti, as might be expected, were received with wonderment near to disbelief, since nothing growing in Europe approached their bizarre appearance, and they were quickly taken up as a hobby by those who could get the few specimens then available. By the middle of the 18th Century, the great Swedish taxonomist Linnaeus had listed only 24 species of cacti, or about 2 per cent of the number known today, in his *Gen-*

era Plantarum, which established modern botanical nomenclature.

Europeans gradually became aware of considerably more than two dozen species. In 1837, James Forbes, who was in charge of the Duke of Bedford's gardens at Woburn Abbey, found extensive collections of cacti in Germany and Belgium, apparently to his great surprise, for the Duke's collection had been assumed to be unequaled anywhere. Forbes swallowed his pride and ordered 200 species each from a Herr Otto of Berlin and a Herr Seitz of Dresden.

A half century later, hundreds of other species were known in Europe. The old man, a columnar cactus which in its native Mexico reaches a height of 50 feet, was shown at the Paris World Exhibition of 1889, where it was advertised as a great rarity and caused a sensation. (So did the Eiffel Tower, which was built for the exhibition and stood more than 900 feet taller than the old man.) The Parisians were so taken with the covering of long, woolly hairs that camouflage its sharp spines that they began a cactus-collecting boom that was halted only by World War I. Hardly had the ink dried on the Armistice, however, before the boom regained its momentum, and Mexico found itself being stripped of its old-man cacti by greedy exporters as wantonly as it had been plundered of its gold some 400 years earlier by the conquistadors. The Mexican government soon passed a law prohibiting the export of all cacti. This action spurred growers to the propagation of cacti from seed, which soon became widely available, and resulted in a happy solution for both Europeans and Mexicans.

In addition to collecting specimens, Europeans were all the while breeding new ones. For example, the genus *Epiphyllum* (the name means "on the leaf") contains some 3,000 hybrids, the first of which was introduced in England in 1839.

If Europeans were slow in taking up the cactus (it took several hundred years for cacti to become popular) consider the case of the average American, who until recently took for granted the availability of the plants within his own country, even though he had never seen most of them. In 1891, with the cactus boom already under way in Europe, a Philadelphia monthly observed that "there are societies nowadays for all sorts of things, but the last thing to be thought of would be a society to encourage the cultivation of cactuses." We have in the intervening years made up for lost time.

By the turn of the century one German grower, Johannes Nicolai of Dresden, had introduced 300 new epiphyllum hybrids all by himself. By 1930, the work had been taken over by Americans in California, and the migrating epiphyllums had come full circle, for they were back near the region where they had originated.

OLD-MAN CACTUS IN PARIS

Cactus blossoms: an enchanting Cinderella story

"Grotesqueness of form or habit is rarely found in combination with floral beauty in the vegetable world," wrote British horticulturist Lewis Castle in 1884. But such combinations do exist and, Castle went on, "no family affords more remarkable examples of this union of widely divergent qualities than the great and peculiar Cactus order." Cactus flowers, oftentimes mounted on prickly pedestals, frequently rival all other flowers for size, fragrance or color.

Day-blooming cactus flowers often rely on striking colors such as glossy reds, oranges and yellows to attract pollinating insects. Night-blooming blossoms generally are a waxy white, employing as a lure a highly potent fragrance reminiscent of vanilla, honeysuckle or hyacinth. Since the plants' period of unfolding is short and often occurs at odd hours, catching cactus blossoms when they are open can be a challenge. If you are busy at work, you may miss the day-blooming plants that shut at sunset, and it is all too easy to sleep through the opening of night-blooming plants that close at dawn. But it is well worth some extra effort to witness cacti in bloom.

Unlike most flowers, cactus blossoms are typically short-stalked and show little difference between sepals and petals. Springing from the areoles of the cacti, the flowers display forms ranging from flat cartwheels to deep funnels. Many blossoms contain hundreds of stamens so sensitive they contract at the slightest touch of an insect.

Easy-to-bloom cacti such as species of mammillaria, notocactus, parodia and rebutia shown on pages 26-29 require only slight attention beyond a basic regimen of eight hours of light a day and occasional watering. Maturing as soon as a year or two in some cases, they will reward you annually with their flowers.

The cacti on pages 30-31 generally take more time to mature and demand extra monitoring. *Melocactus matanzanus*, for example, will bloom only after four or five years of careful cultivation, temperatures that never drop below 60° and enough soil for a large root system. In time, even the most reluctant cacti can be coaxed to show their true colors as the Cinderellas of the plant kingdom.

Gymnocalycium damsii's multipetaled flowers bloom readily in the spring and may last up to a week indoors. The 2-inch blossoms range from pink to white.

Flowers without fuss

MAMMILLARIA CHINOCEPHALA
Given bright sunlight, these flowers blossom readily.

NOTOCACTUS LENINGHAUSII
This cactus grows slowly, but flowers in its youth.

26

MAMMILLARIA PROLIFERA
*A veritable bouquet of blooms can be
expected from this plant.*

NEOPORTERIA NIDUS
*Early flowering, this cactus unfolds its
large blossoms as early as February.*

MAMMILLARIA WILDII
*This free-flowering species needs only a
short dormancy period.*

REBUTIA SENILIS
These funnel-shaped flowers bloom readily in the springtime.

MAMMILLARIA ZEPHYRANTHOIDES
Unlike most mammillarias, this cactus bears large flowers.

NOTOCACTUS HERTERI
This hardy cactus will flower under harsh climatic conditions.

PARODIA CHRYSACANTHION
These vivid flowers emerge surprisingly early in the spring of the year.

NOTOCACTUS OTTONIS BRASILIENSIS
This cactus' bright, 2-inch blossoms open only during the daytime.

Color that needs coaxing

ECHINOCEREUS PENTALOPHUS
A strictly enforced regimen of sunlight will help this plant to grow and flower.

WILCOXIA POSELGERI
If it can be kept strong—by staking or grafting it to another cactus—this plant will flower.

NEOPORTERIA ARMATUS
*Highly susceptible to rot, this species must
be kept nearly dry to ensure good health.*

THELOCACTUS BICOLOR
*Strong light is needed to induce these
3-inch-wide flowers to appear.*

MELOCACTUS MATANZANUS
*These cacti often require four or five years
of cultivation before they bloom.*

31

House guests that make few demands 2

Happily for gardeners with limited outdoor space or an inhospitable winter climate, many cacti and other succulents need only a place in the sun to thrive—even a tiny window sill will do. Some succulents, in fact, can make do with little sun, but most require at least four hours exposure a day. You are courting disaster, or at least the disappointment of never seeing your succulents in bloom, if you raise them in surroundings that do not satisfy this modest need.

One succulent that will grow well without any direct sunlight at all is the sansevieria, or snake plant, and thus it is not surprising to see its clumps of mottled green spikes, which look rather like inverted sabers, providing generous masses of dazzling greenery on north-facing window sills. Growing most other succulents in such gloomy surroundings, however, requires the use of artificial light.

Depending upon the amount of available growing space, you can raise succulents in a simply staggering range of sizes—from the tiny baby toes to the towering 65-foot columnar cereus. The fascinating baby toes, a native of southern Africa, hides underground, showing only a half inch or so of its flattened tips. These tips are translucent and serve the same function as windows: they admit light, enabling the plant to feed itself despite the fact that most of it is cut off from the sun's rays. Baby toes understandably needs steady and strong light; without it, the plant simply disappears into the soil and eventually dies. Some gardeners pot baby toes so that most of the plant is exposed to ensure that it gets enough light.

From the negligible height of the baby toes the succulent fancier enters a world of increasingly larger specimens. However, at a time when the acceptable height of a residential ceiling seems to be descending precipitously, few indoor gardeners are likely to have much use for outsize plants, and unless you have a private ballroom, you ought to limit your acquaintance with the family giants to those growing outdoors in the Southwest, where they can be admired in all

Light-hungry succulents thrive in a Pennsylvania window where a southeast exposure gives hours of sun daily. Vigor is sustained in winter with artificial light, in summer by moving the plants outdoors.

their glory. There are, nonetheless, many reasonably tall cacti, such as the organ pipe, that can be grown in the most cramped apartment. If you have your heart set on a giant saguaro, be of good cheer. Potting a saguaro generally stops it from developing the wide-ranging root system it requires to increase in size. In any event, it may take these monsters 10 years to grow to a height of 4 inches in their native habitat, and 250 years to reach 50 feet. Should your potted saguaro appear to be headed toward its full natural size, you can donate it to the nearest botanical garden and settle for its little cousin, the old-man cactus that so delighted Parisians a century ago.

LET IT DRAIN   Whether your collection revolves around several spectacular saguaros or is built on a more modest scale with smaller succulents, the way the plants are potted can spell the difference between failure and success. The best home away from home for a cactus or other succulent is a clay pot with a large drainage hole at its bottom. The porous clay allows roots to get the air they need. Nonporous plastic pots retain moisture, which is fine for ferns but potentially lethal for succulents, since too much moisture may initiate rot at the roots and undersides of the plants. Thus, if you have a succulent in a plastic container, it should be transplanted to a clay pot as quickly as possible, without disturbing the soil around the roots.

Whether it is new or has previously housed one of your own plants, a clay pot should be well scrubbed with soap and hot water. If some of your clay pots are badly cracked or chipped, do not throw them away. Instead, break off large pieces and place them over the drainage holes of your usable pots. With a hammer, crush the remaining portions of the cracked pots into gravel-like bits to be used as drainage layers. To avoid flying chips and clouds of dust, wrap the shards in an old towel before crushing them. Of course, if you have no broken pots to smash, layers of gravel will do.

A MIX TO GROW ON   The classic cactus soil consists of equal parts of commercial potting soil, rich in humus, and sand to improve drainage. Vermiculite or perlite can be substituted for the sand, or these gritty materials can be mixed. Particles of charcoal will help keep the mix from becoming too acid. If you mix cactus soil, use coarse builder's sand; ocean-beach sand is too salty. Pasteurize any homemade soil mixture by heating it in an oven at 250° for at least half an hour.

As you might gather just from looking at it, repotting a cactus, particularly a large one, is a tricky business and requires a bit of advance preparation. If you have ever tugged fruitlessly at a barbed glochid embedded in your fingertip, you are already aware of the need to plan ahead. Wear leather gloves and have a pair of tongs ready, as well as a rag or rolled-up newspaper, using them to hold the plant in position while you are pouring the soil mixture over its roots. Tamp the soil frequently with the blunt end of the tongs.

Do not water a newly repotted cactus or other succulent immediately, even though your experience with other plants has made immediate watering practically a reflex action. A succulent should be given a rest of at least a week after a change of pot before it is watered. Very young plants are exceptions; their soil needs to be dampened immediately after repotting.

Fortunately, most succulents are very slow growers and will need to be repotted only every three years or so, since they will exhaust the soil before they outgrow the confines of the containers. Add a teaspoonful of bone meal in the spring to average-sized pots (4 to 8 inches in diameter) until the plants have attained such dimensions that they appear to be crying out for repotting. A plant will be most comfortable in its container if it has a band of about 1 inch of soil around it.

The key word to bear in mind when watering cacti is restraint; enough of them to fill the Mojave Desert have probably been turned to mush by overwatering. As you wield the watering can, remember that some cacti are already 95 per cent water and can hold out even if you miss a visit or two. In winter, when most cacti are dormant, once a month is enough for all but those in the smallest pots (2 inches or less). The only point of watering at all in winter is to keep the plants from shriveling so much they become unsightly. The rest of the year, a cactus is actively growing and will need water about once a week. If the plant is very young, however, it may need water two or three times a week. Conditions such as excessive dryness or high temperature may also make more frequent watering necessary. The best way to tell if cacti and other succulents are getting enough water is to study their appearance: they should be plump and well filled with water. If they are puckered, increase their water ration, wetting the soil thoroughly each time. If the pot is standing in a saucer, pour off any water that drains through.

Other succulents generally require watering twice as frequently as cacti—two or three times a week in summer, twice a month in winter, though your own experience will ultimately acquaint you with the best watering schedule for each particular plant.

Poking the soil with your finger to test its dryness, a valuable aid in judging when to water most plants, is a useful guide with succulents, but a dry feel does not necessarily mean the plant must be watered; it may indicate only that your soil is draining well. If your soil is not draining quickly enough or remains soggy, repot the plant in a mixture of 1 part commercial potting soil and 1 part sand.

PAPERING OVER A PRICKLY JOB

A prickly cactus can be easily moved to a new pot with the aid of a sling of rolled newspaper. First, cover the drainage hole of the new pot with a crockery shard and line the bottom third of the pot with gravel and an inch or more of soil. Tap the bottom of the old pot on a hard surface to loosen the soil, then wrap the cactus in the sling and lift it out. Place it in the new pot so the soil line on the plant is ½ inch below the rim of the pot and fill around the root ball with potting mix. Do not water for a week.

Once your cacti and succulents have been properly potted and you have established a congenial watering schedule, there is little else for you to do but keep your plants clean and free of pests and diseases. One of the banes of a succulent fancier's existence is rot, which usually appears at the base of the plant as a black, discolored patch, behind which is soft, pulpy plant tissue. A grapefruit spoon, with its serrated tip, is the perfect instrument for removing rot, and the succulent grower soon learns to have one around even if he does not like grapefruit. To remove diseased tissue, scrape it away with the spoon and dust the wound with powdered sulfur to prevent further infection, then sterilize the spoon. The plant will eventually grow a tough new skin, called a callus, over the wound. Treat rot due to overwatering the same way as rot caused by infections.

SAP-SUCKING MEALY BUGS

Though their tough skins discourage pests, cacti and succulents are not immune to them by any means. Probably the most dangerous insect enemies of succulents are mealy bugs, which look like small tufts of cotton that have somehow alighted on your plants. Under the white tufts are waxy shells that make the insects particularly difficult to eradicate. If they are not picked off the plants, they will suck the sap out and leave trails of sticky honeydew. To get rid of mealy bugs, dislodge them with a toothpick or kill them by applying alcohol to them with a cotton swab. Remove mealy bugs as

PICKING THE PERFECT POT

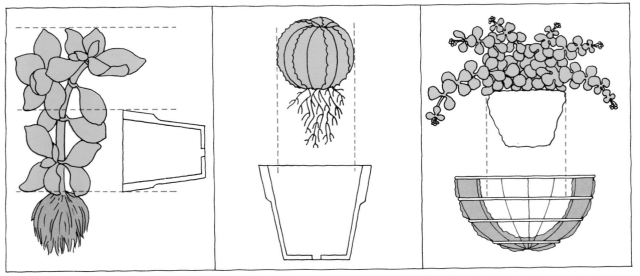

Succulents that are potted in oversized or undersized containers look awkward and may not prosper. As a rule of thumb, pot a tall plant in a container that is half as wide as the height of the plant.

Ball-shaped succulents usually grow best in containers that fit them with very little room to spare. Pot a round succulent in a container with a diameter that is only one inch wider than the width of the plant.

Hanging wire baskets for succulents must be large enough to accommodate the lining of sphagnum moss that contains the soil. Generally, such a basket should be 4 inches wider than the plant's root ball.

soon as you spot them, since all the ants in the neighborhood will come to feast on the honeydew provided by the creatures and will transport them to other plants.

If the infestation has gotten out of hand, use a pyrethrum-rotenone spray. (Rotenone is derived from the roots of cubé, a tropical plant; pyrethrum is processed from some species of chrysanthemums.) Spray outside wherever possible; if you must spray inside, do so near an open window.

Two other sucking pests that attack succulents are aphids, which resemble minute grasshoppers, and scales, which look like tiny dots, usually brown, and tend to cluster around the areoles of cacti. To remove either, scrub the plant gently with soapy water and rinse it. If they persist, bring on the pyrethrum-rotenone mixture.

The root nematode, or rootworm, is a particularly insidious pest because it wreaks its havoc unseen in the succulent's roots. The first visible signs of damage on the plant usually are a pronounced pallor and a marked slowing of growth. When these occur, unearth the roots and examine them for suspicious swellings; if any are found, cut them off with a sharp, sterile knife. The remaining roots should be exposed to fresh air for a week and then repotted in fresh soil.

The only other housekeeping chore required of the succulent keeper is the cutting away of dead and dying portions, always at the nearest joint uniting them to the main body of the plant. Though it is not common practice to pinch succulents to force more flowering, underachieving portions should promptly be removed to provide less crowded growing conditions for more assertive branches or leaves.

There cannot be many people who have not owned a succulent, at least one of the common ones, since they are widely sold in such places as card shops and supermarkets, where they are impulse items—something you did not plan to buy but could not resist.

Succulents are obviously less perishable than fresh vegetables or baked goods, but they are not as hardy as toys and paperweights, and in some of these unlikely plant emporiums—and even in some plant shops—the clerks do not seem to realize that succulents must be watered occasionally. Lighting in these shops may be inadequate for a stay of more than a few days for a succulent, especially if the plants have already spent some time in shipping cartons. Check each succulent—whether a supermarket jade plant or a florist-shop opuntia—for a healthy appearance and an absence of insects or rot. You cannot unpot the plants to look for root nematodes, but a sharp eye can usually detect any rot around the soil line.

Examine any large and expensive plant closely to be sure its roots are well developed and that it has not simply been unearthed

THE WARY BUYER'S GUIDE

from the wild, thrown into a pot and rushed to market. To accomplish this examination without uprooting the succulent, simply press firmly against it while gripping the rim of the pot: if the plant does not wobble, the roots are probably well established.

GARDENS BY MAIL ORDER

An exciting and easy way of acquiring unusual succulents is to order them through the catalogues of Texas, California and Arizona growers. These are as tempting to succulent fanciers as more general seed catalogues are to the average gardener. One Columbus, Ohio, grower calls his catalogue a cactus wish book. Winter purchases are often sent at the customer's risk, since the plants may freeze during shipment, so it is better to wait for spring before ordering. Mail-order plants commonly are shipped with bare roots or unpotted. Upon their arrival they should be repotted like any succulent. One advantage of receiving plants with bare roots is that they can be easily checked for rot and nematodes. No shipper knowingly sends defective plants if they are going to arrive with all their troubles thoroughly exposed.

If you should chance to be in cactus country and are tempted with the thought that no one would miss one or two of the many beautiful specimens seemingly yours for the taking, think again. In the opinion of many experts, cacti are the most endangered of all plants: one fourth of the native species in the United States are on the verge of extinction. The reason for this sad condition is that most cacti—unlike the opuntia that abounds uncontrollably practically anywhere—will grow naturally only in limited areas where conditions are exactly right for their special needs. When those limited areas are disturbed, the cacti can no longer survive.

DESERT LOOTERS BEWARE

In Arizona, a special police force patrols desert areas to keep botanical bootleggers from stealing cacti. Other destructive forces that imperil the cactus include fire (particularly the brush fires of Southern California), uncontrolled livestock grazing and indiscriminate construction. Florida's Everglades National Park, for example, is one of only two places in the United States where four particular genera of cacti are found, and the drainage and pollution accompanying construction are threatening the area where they grow.

Apart from ethical and moral considerations, there are practical reasons for not participating in the pillage of cacti, and the chief of these is that your plunder will probably not survive, particularly if you are going to change drastically the circumstances under which it will live. The soil requirements of many cacti are incredibly exacting and it is the rare hobbyist who is able to meet them.

If you must have a native cactus to take home with you, it is far wiser, and an act of kindness to future generations of people and cacti, to take a cutting, or better still to gather some seeds and grow your own *(page 79)*. You will need permission from the landowner or local authorities to make such a harvest, of course. Cacti are extremely prodigal with their seed; the common Southwestern barrel cactus produces some 1,500 seeds in each pod, and as many as 25,000 on one plant. The seeds you help yourself to, unlike the plants that produced them, will not be missed.

Whether you buy, grow or otherwise collect cactus, the specimens can be displayed in your home in striking ways. For example, a sunny corner in one of your rooms can be filled with succulents, which need not be large or expensive. Such a collection is always more attractive if you place a large plant or two at the back of the group and progressively smaller plants in front of them. The number of plants in your display depends upon the size of the room; when in doubt use only stellar specimens and put the runners-up somewhere else. The finalists will look and grow better if they are not crowded.

You can give a cactus-and-succulent display an added fillip by housing it in what essentially is an indoor sandbox, its height determined by the tallest pot in the grouping. This container can be built of scrap wood, the more weathered the better, since the aged boards will suggest what will ultimately become a desert landscape. Line the box with a sheet of plastic to prevent water seepage.

Place the plants inside the container in their own pots, and fill the areas between them with sand or soil. If your display is a large one, you can cut down on the amount of sand needed by sandwiching crumpled newspaper between the plants and covering it with yet another sheet of plastic. Cut openings for pots in the top sheet, arrange them in the box and cover the plastic with a layer of sand for a convincing bit of desert scenery in your living room. You can add further verisimilitude by strewing the sand with rocks and patches of gravel. Such a succulent sandbox need not be a lavish production to be eye-catching, especially if your space is limited. It can be effective if it is contained in a deep roasting pan on a window sill.

The ultimate minilandscape is the dish garden. Many types of plants can be used in it, but succulents are particularly apt candidates: they grow so slowly that a carefully arranged composition may last two or three years before the plants must be repotted. Furthermore, there is a virtual army of small succulents, many in bizarre shapes, that can turn a dish landscape into a work of art.

Some excellent containers for dish gardens are probably buried deep in the recesses of your kitchen cupboards: a slightly faded and crazed pottery bowl, a plastic silverware tray or a mismatched teacup that you were ready to throw out. Even a clay drainage

EASING A HANDFUL OF PAIN

Even veteran cactus growers have to deal with an occasional finger full of spines or glochids. Spines are removed like splinters, though with greater ease, since they do not break. Pull out a spine with a pair of sterilized tweezers, then wash the affected area with soap and warm water. To remove glochids, which are practically invisible once embedded, cover the skin with a thin coating of rubber cement. When the cement has dried, rub it off, and the glochids will be pulled free. Cellophane tape may be used instead of rubber cement.

DESERT IN A DISH

saucer 2 inches deep will accommodate a collection of tiny succulents and provide a natural and unobtrusive background as well.

The incipient dish garden should be lined with a layer of gravel for drainage, since most such containers have no drainage holes. Those that leak are even better for succulent gardens than those that do not. Place a thin layer of crushed charcoal over the gravel. This will act as a soil purifier and will foster a better chemical balance in the soil, but it will not promote growth, an estimable trait, since your objective is to keep the plants healthy but small.

An extraordinary succulent dish garden can be composed solely of echeverias with plump rosettes of varying sizes—from the tiny-leaved *E. expatriata,* which also produces tiny pink flowers, to the *E. elegans,* with somewhat larger leaves that are pure white.

You can create a more varied grouping by placing a chunk of rock in the center of the container and grading the soil down gently to its outer edges. In this setting, you can combine echeverias with lithops, which look like split rocks (flowers may appear in the clefts); haworthias, with tiny zebra-striped leaves; or any other miniatures you wish to incorporate. Do not try to cram your dish garden with plants: those that are sparsely planted are not only more convincing as replicas of nature but offer better growing conditions for their inhabitants. Some of the spaces between succulents can be filled with trails of gravel or bits of rock and bark, arranged to suggest a natural scene such as a dry riverbed.

CRADLED IN FEATHER ROCK

A dramatic and salubrious container for a dish garden can be made of predrilled volcanic rock, sometimes called feather rock because it is so surprisingly light. The pale gray and brown tones of the material, as well as its ragged texture and naturally craggy contours, evoke the sheer rock faces of the Grand Canyon or the majestic masses of Monument Valley. Succulents blend with sublime ease into these little rock gardens and when well planted look as though they had been scooped off the desert floor already growing. Predrilled rock is widely available at plant stores and garden centers. Wear gloves whenever you handle it: the material consists basically of glass in its crudest form, and you can receive a nasty gash merely by brushing your hand against it.

Before planting a predrilled rock, place a half inch of sand or gravel at the bottom of the hole and, since your succulents will be growing in very little soil, fill it with a cactus mixture to which you have added some bone meal (half a teaspoon to a cup) as a nutrient. A top layer of sand will help forestall rot.

Your indoor rock garden should be kept on a tray of some sort, for although the amount of water used in succulent care is small compared to that used for other plants, there is always the possibility you will overwater, particularly on the first few tries, and the excess may seep onto floors and furniture. A glass pie plate filled with gravel makes a harmonious and unobtrusive tray.

An equally handsome and only slightly less long-lived container for a succulent planting can be made by hollowing a naturally bleached piece of driftwood or a length of weathered beam. In the Southwest, tourists are offered cactus gardens in containers made from the woody ribs of the giant saguaro. Though you may not have saguaro ribs around, you can find vessels for original dish gardens at such places as demolition sites or rocky outcroppings in the countryside, where you may find all manner of suitable natural materials.

Succulents need not be earthbound, and if you are running out of floor space for them and have a window that admits suitable amounts of light, tie leather thongs or ropes to your pots and hang them from well-secured ceiling hooks, for an indoor cactus garden takes on a different and fascinating perspective floating in air. You can buy elaborate macramé hangers if you like, but do not choose the kind that are so elaborate that they detract from the plant. Succulents with drooping branches such as the rattail cactus are effective in hanging baskets, and those with even a slight trailing habit, such as the Christmas cactus, grow better aloft, since the tips of their branches will not be trailing on a tabletop. The Christmas cactus grows by adding claw-shaped stem segments, so it may be called the crab cactus, a name that seems even more appropriate.

Some succulents are so pendulous of habit that they should be grown only in hanging baskets. These include such sedums as the burro's tail, whose plump green leaves are tightly clustered along the trailing stems; the carpet sedums, both variegated and nonvariegated; and possibly the most beautiful sedum of all, the ghost plant, whose intricately twisted and ever downward-thrusting stems are covered with echeveria-like rosettes of palest silvery green flushed with blue. Despite its ethereal beauty, the ghost plant is tough, and will survive not only neglect but downright abuse.

A hanging basket is only a pot to which wires have been attached; plants to be grown in one should be potted exactly as are their earthbound fellows. One of the fringe benefits of suspending succulents instead of more familiar plants is that there will be fewer occasions when you must get up on a chair or ladder to water and fewer times when you will have to wipe up spills below. Though these are hardly compelling reasons for growing succulents, you will find them a comfort when you realize that your plantkeeping chores are taking less time than you expected.

A DROWN-PROOF DISH GARDEN

To avoid overwatering a dish garden that lacks a drainage hole, insert a ½- to 1-inch-diameter plastic tube into the soil to the depth of the bottom drainage layer. Conceal the tube with a stone. Check the tube a few hours after watering; no water should remain. If it does, insert one end of a cotton cord into the tube, putting the other end in a small bowl placed lower than the container. The cord will slowly draw excess water into the bowl. For quick removal, use a kitchen baster to draw off the excess.

Hanging your succulents in the window a few inches away from the glass allows you to take maximum advantage of available light. Almost any succulent can be grown in the strong light of a southern exposure, but if your only available window faces north, you will have to content yourself with the snake plant, which you may as well set on the sill since it will never trail and might otherwise scrape the ceiling. If you have windows facing east or west, you can grow succulents like the orchid cactus, since it is not a full sun-worshipper; it will trail generously over the sides of its basket. The flowers resemble enormous camellias more than they do orchids, and you have a choice of some 3,000 varieties. The mistletoe cactus will also thrive in less than full sun and will grace your window for months with the tiny berries that succeed its small flowers.

EAST OR WEST MAY BE BEST

There are other succulents that will thrive in the limited sunlight of eastern (sun in the morning) and western (afternoon only) exposures, even if they are not hung in your windows. One of the most interesting of these is the lobivia; the name is derived from Bolivia, where it was discovered, spelled not quite backward. Lobivia flowers encompass a vast range of delicate colors and have the endearing habit of forming perfect circles with their fellows.

Compatible with the lobivia under conditions of less than day-long sunlight are the agave cactus, which produces yellow flowers; the Christmas, Easter and Thanksgiving cacti; and the pencil euphorbia, which despite its name is on occasion tipped with tiny flower sprigs rather than sharp points. Like other euphorbias, it contains a secretion that may be irritating, and it should be washed off if it gets onto your skin. Though the list of succulents that will survive in less than full sunlight is by no means endless, it is long enough so that there is some choice even for gardeners who cannot provide perfect light conditions.

REGIMEN FOR FLOWERING

Most succulents will flower if they receive the required temperature, light and dark during dormancy *(Chapter 5)* and are fertilized with bone meal once a month during their growing season. Bone meal contains five times as much phosphorus as nitrogen and stimulates the growth of flowers rather than leaves. Keep your succulents cool (50° to 55°) during the winter, water only when their soil becomes very dry, and they should reward your patient care with blossoms the following spring.

The Christmas cactus needs a specilized regimen if it is to flower for the festive season. Like the poinsettia, it must have absolute darkness from dusk to dawn beginning in late September and ending in early December or when the buds have formed. A common method of meeting this requirement is to put it in a closet or some other place where no lights are likely to be turned on at night, but you must remember to return the plant to the sun daily. Some cactus fanciers simply place a box over each plant; if the plant is hanging, you can cover it with a lightproof shroud, rather as you would cover a canary cage to keep the bird quiet.

Keep the plant dry, cool and unfed until buds form. When they do, resume normal watering, feed the plants small quantities of bone meal monthly and put your shrouds and boxes away. With seasonal adjustments, the same treatment applies for other celebratory species: Easter cacti go into the dark in late January, Thanksgiving cacti three months before the turkey goes into the oven.

Getting larger specimens to flower often requires artificial light, since the light that comes into even a sunny room provides only a fraction of the 10,000 or more foot-candles they might be basking in out in the desert. A practical way of boosting their light diet is to suspend 150-watt incandescent plant lights a few feet above them. These bulbs have built-in reflectors and can be used in ordinary incandescent sockets if you happen to have them in the right places.

Some gardeners turn up their noses at the idea of succulents under light, claiming that they never look as well as those grown under natural conditions, but constant progress in lighting equipment and energetic experimentation by growers have produced such heartening results that no one who admires succulents need live without them. Nor do you have to be an electrician to cope with artificial light, despite the existence of a bewildering choice of bulbs and tubes with formidably technical names. Crown-of-thorns, for example, will reward you with its salmon-colored flowers by the light of an ordinary fluorescent fixture containing two 40-watt tubes. Keep the plant about 6 inches from the center of the tubes, where it will get the light it needs to do its best. Crown-of-thorns does not even need controlled periods of darkness to flower, as does the Christmas cactus, so it can be brought into bloom in a living room.

Doubling the number of tubes will result in greatly increased possibilities for bringing succulents into bloom. Four 40-watt tubes deliver approximately 1,000 foot-candles to plants 6 inches below them, enough light to bring furry panda plants into flower. These require a month of 10-hour days two months before blooming, which occurs 10 months after the seeds germinate. After flowering, they can go gradually back to a conventional 16-hour day. As for other plants, even if they do not bloom, you can count on good growth under artificial light. These include jade plants, peanut cacti and many other succulents. Perhaps to have these exotic plants growing at all under indoor light conditions is paradise enough.

UNDER AN ARTIFICIAL SUN

Inviting the desert into your home

Both shaped by and shaping the Western wilderness, cacti and succulents are so much a part of that vast landscape that their careful arrangement in indoor gardens, whether in a thimbleful of sand or planted wall-to-wall, can conjure up images of towering saguaros and big barrel cacti. The forms that such a patch of cactus country may take are limited only by space; not only can a great number of succulent species be grown readily indoors, but the plant bed and surrounding room can echo the desert's colors, textures and shapes.

Because cacti and succulents tend to grow slowly, an interior desert landscape may endure for years to come. Given fast-draining soil, the dry air common to most homes nowadays and plenty of sunlight, some species will even reach the same height and flower as profusely as their kin in the wild. Most importantly for the over-worked gardener, many have such similar horticultural needs that taking care of them indoors is almost child's play.

Where space is at a premium, a Lilliputian dish garden *(opposite and pages 46-47)* provides a desert scene striking in its tiny scale and sculptural form. Many slow-growing succulents are ideal for dish gardens, since the plants need larger quarters only every two or three years at the most. Dish gardens can boast a saving in money as well as space, as one enthusiast explains: "I can create in a dish garden for a few dollars what a wealthier person might create for several thousand dollars on a couple of acres."

On a somewhat more extensive scale, light-loving succulents can fill an entire window sill; the copper-lined planter on page 32 is strewn with pebbles between the plants, echoing a desert vista and making the setting seem far larger than its 3½-by-7-foot size. A similar space-stretching effect can be achieved by setting off the desert tones of a modern interior with a few large succulents in pots resembling boulders *(pages 48-49)*. The most ambitious indoor gardeners can complete the picture with actual desert materials and a walk-through roomful of cacti and succulents such as those that are growing in the spectacular home hothouse on pages 50-51.

Safely sheltered from a winter snowfall in Pennsylvania, a spiky Crassula perforata towers above a dozen other succulents and cacti in a 13-inch desert dish garden.

The littlest landscape

Building a dramatic dish garden for cacti and succulents is like putting together a doll house: by grouping plants that need similar care and relate to each other in Lilliputian perspective just as larger varieties do in the wild, the gardener creates a miniature mirror of the desert. The only special tools needed are those one resourceful practitioner turned to when she traded her spade for a spoon and her watering can for an eyedropper.

A miniature rock garden, dominated by a large purple aeonium surrounded by echeverias, has prospered for two years in this 16-inch clay saucer. The sterile planting mix has equal parts of potting soil, sharp sand and perlite.

These thumb-sized gardens are watered only once every two weeks to limit growth. The largest, crowned by a bushy Cereus peruvianus, is six years old; the thimble plants will not need repotting for a year.

Towering over 1- and 2-inch succulents, a 7-inch Opuntia maranae creates the illusion of a full-sized desert scene.

Shades of the old West

Often striking in their sculptural domination of the Western land-scape, large cacti and succulents can set the stage for a symbolic re-creation of arid countryside in a desert-like interior of coordinated colors and shapes. Seemingly sun-bleached shades of sandy tans and grays on walls, floors and furniture, coupled with solid, simple forms for pots, pillows and other furnishings, will keep huge desert denizens from appearing out of place even in an urban living room.

Complemented by boulder-like pillows and planters and desert colors, great euphorbias and other succulents turn a New York room into a rare setting: an indoor garden comfortable for people as well as plants. These large specimens require the strong sunlight they get from southern and eastern exposures.

Heading for the best roundup

For the ultimate in indoor cactus and succulent gardens, adventurous growers can condense the landscape of the desert into a single sunlit room with hillocks, pathways and plants forming a Western panorama fit for a Hollywood set. Careful attention must be paid to soil and climate conditions, but if you can provide a hothouse environment that simulates the weather in the West, you can have a true desert view in any area of the country.

An extraordinary indoor cactus and succulent garden on Long Island harbors about 2,000 species in semiarid splendor. Provided with a complete sun roof and a 35-by-50-foot roomful of sandy soil, the succulents not only grow vigorously but also reward the gardener with unfailing flowering.

An exotic garden for any climate 3

Succulents bring to the outdoor garden the same virtues that they possess indoors—flamboyant flowers grown rather effortlessly on bizarrely handsome plants—and since some are hardy enough to stand temperatures as low as 40° below zero, they have a place in almost every garden from New Mexico to Saskatchewan.

The outdoor succulent garden can easily be brought eastward, especially to the Gulf Coast area, although many species of cacti must stay in their native desert because they cannot stand intense humidity. This is hardly cause for dismay, however, since there are many species that will not only thrive in the East but also produce flowers just as splendid as those of their desert relations.

A profusely flowering cactus that thrives in high humidity is the queen-of-the-night cactus, which bears large white night-blooming flowers and frequently forms large colonies as it scrambles over the ground or climbs up walls and fences. Another warm-weather cactus, called the fragrant harrisia, produces large and, as you might expect from its name, odoriferous blossoms, and bears orange fruit somewhat like that of the prickly pear.

Many subtropical succulent gardeners sing the praises of the silver-crown cotyledon, a shrub about 3 feet high that has ruffled white leaves, and the purple aeonium, a black-leaved succulent of about the same height. As a ground cover, one crassula, string-of-buttons, will twist its matched pairs of leaves, which appear to be endlessly strung to each other, generously underfoot in your garden.

In rainy and warm regions, a fast-draining soil is essential for growing succulents, and water must have a place to drain away from moisture-sensitive root systems. If possible, choose a sloping site, but if necessary you can provide proper drainage by creating sloping beds where none exist naturally. Begin by digging out the bed to a depth of at least 6 inches; fill the excavation with rocks, broken bricks or old masonry. If you have a mixture of materials, use the

Unbowed beneath a blanket of melting snow, a yellow-fruited cane cholla (Opuntia spinosior) ignores the ravages of winter in central Arizona. It grows to 8 or 10 feet tall in outdoor gardens of the Southwest.

rubble on the bottom and the rocks in the top layer, so some of them can protrude. Limestone is particularly good for this purpose because it will also help to keep the bed alkaline, as cacti accustomed to the alkaline soil found in arid regions prefer. Finally, add a mixture of 1 part soil, 2 parts sand and 1 part humus or leaf mold to form a fast-draining mound (page 55). Succulents growing in rainy regions will need a more nourishing soil than those in arid areas, so add ½ cup of bone meal for each gallon of the planting mix, but their care is otherwise the same. Watering is necessary only in dry spells.

COLD-CLIMATE CACTI

Gardeners who live in cooler regions of the country do not usually attempt outdoor cactus plantings. Some people perhaps reason that a sudden uncommon outcropping of cacti in the suburbs of northern cities might appear incongruous. Many northerners, though, probably just do not know that many hardy cacti exist, since they are not widely visible or available. Yet cacti can be artfully blended into the northern landscape, which is, after all, what nature itself does. Beachgoers and boating enthusiasts in the New York area are not astonished to see the wild yellow-flowered *Opuntia humifusa* mingling freely with beach roses and marsh grass along the shores of Long Island Sound. The northern gardener can, with equal subtlety, introduce a bed of hardy cacti into a garden or keep several plants in containers outdoors the year round without upstaging the garden's other inhabitants.

There is not, to be sure, a great variety of hardy cacti and other succulents available to the northern gardener, but there is certainly enough to tempt you to try your hand. There are, for example, at least a dozen hardy species of prickly pear ranging in height from that of a blade of grass to that of a medium-sized tree, an equal number of hardy sedums to use as ground covers, a great number of sempervivums and several hedgehog cacti with flowers of almost blindingly brilliant colors.

THE DROWNING DANGER

A fast-draining soil is even more crucial in the northern succulent garden than it is in the warmer regions of the country. Without it, the combination of cold and wetness will destroy the roots of any cactus and many other succulents. To provide the best possible drainage for your plants, make a bed as described on page 55, except that you should add 1 part gravel to the basic planting mix to make it drain even faster. Cacti grown outdoors in the north should also be mulched with pebbles, which are both useful and decorative. They will reflect warmth from the sun to the plants, and will also help to keep the bases of the plants dry.

Gardeners unaccustomed to working with outdoor cacti should not be alarmed to see their plants begin to shrivel as winter ap-

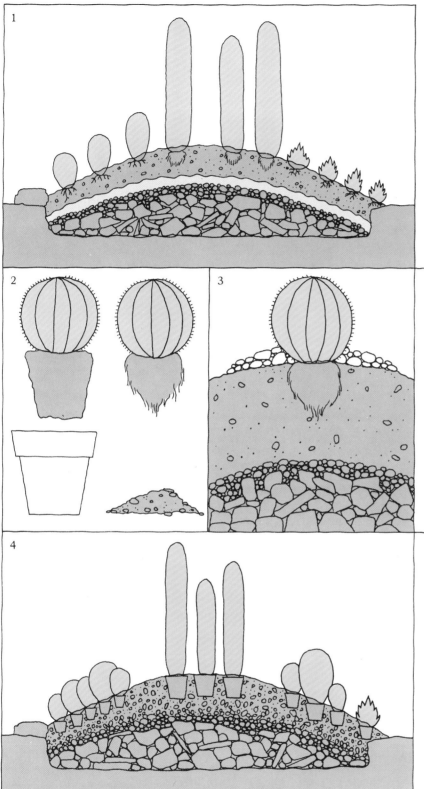

A WELL-DRAINED BED

1. *For a permanent outdoor cactus garden, excavate a sunny bed to a depth of at least 6 inches and add a pile of rocks or broken bricks about a foot high. Slope the sides to ensure fast drainage. Fill crannies and cover the pile with 2 or 3 inches of gravel. Then add a 1-inch layer of coarse sand. Finish the bed with 6 to 8 inches of a mixture of 1 part topsoil, 1 part leaf mold and 2 parts sand. For faster drainage, add 1 part gravel.*

2. *Remove the largest plant you will be using from its pot. Very gently brush as much soil as possible from its roots without damaging them.*

3. *Dig a hole at the top of the bed and place the plant in it at the same level at which it was growing in the pot. Firm the soil and surround the plant with a collar of pebbles to reflect sunlight and prevent rot. Plant the other specimens, working from the top center of the bed to the bottom edge. Leave ample space between plants for good ventilation. After planting, dampen the soil, then do not water again for a week.*

4. *If your winter is too cold or wet for the cacti and succulents you have collected to survive outdoors, construct a bed of rubble covered with a fast-draining mixture of half sand and half gravel. When dependably warm weather arrives, sink potted plants up to their rims in the sandy mixture, after they have been a week in light shade and a week in full sun for half days, to adjust to the outdoors. A plant that has been growing in the strong light of a window facing south should be oriented so the side that faced south indoors also faces south outdoors; otherwise it may die of sunburn.*

proaches. Indeed, some will keel over and play dead until spring. This phenomenon occurs because the plants reduce their water content as a protection against freezing. Northern gardeners need not become upset, either, at the sight of a light covering of snow, which is actually beneficial to the plants, though heavy accumulations that threaten to break a cactus should be brushed away.

Despite the visible dormancy of its denizens, the succulent garden does not present a dreary appearance in winter, and is surely a less dispiriting sight than last summer's vegetable or flower garden. It is, instead, of a piece with other areas of the garden where trees and shrubs have retreated into themselves and are awaiting the return to active growth signaled by spring.

A SUMMER OUTDOORS   Northern gardeners who are unwilling to subject their cacti, however hardy, to the blasts of winter, or who simply prefer to enjoy them as indoor potted plants during cold weather, can compromise by moving the entire collection to the superior growing conditions outdoors when mild weather sets in. An indoor collection must be acclimatized gradually to bright sunlight—a week in partial shade, a week of half days in the sun, then full sun. If you are moving only a few potted succulents outdoors, simply dig holes larger than the pots and sink the pots to their rims in gravel. For a larger collection of such plants, make a mound of rubble, sand and gravel *(page 55),* then dig holes large enough to accommodate the pots and sink them to their rims. Your succulents should be placed just as they would be in an indoor display, with the tallest specimens toward the back of your bed and the smaller ones toward the front, where they will be visible from the house, so that you may enjoy them from indoors even while you are busy washing dishes or cleaning windows.

A semblance of permanence can be achieved by filling in the spaces between the pots with gravel and a few larger stones to create an approximation of the surroundings in which desert cacti grow. Choose a spot for this temporary planting that receives full sun for at least half a day and enjoys good drainage. A patch of yard where the grass grows sparsely is a good place for this grouping, as are the ragged edges of driveways and walks. If your containers are not eyesores and you prefer not to sink them into the soil, arrange them in an attractive grouping. Some growers keep hardy cacti outdoors all year long aboveground in clay pots filled only with gravel. One cactus that responds well to such treatment is the California grizzly bear, one of the prickly pears, which has enormous 4-inch flowers and is very spiny. It can safely be left outdoors for the winter.

You can have a modest and practically foolproof version of a cold-weather cactus garden simply by putting your potted plants in a redwood window box or planter against a sheltered but sunny side of the house. In a time of proliferating redwood structures, the container may even appear to be part of the house itself. The planter should contain a half-and-half mixture of sand and gravel around the pots, as well as plenty of drainage holes.

Housing for your outdoor cactus collection is not limited to redwood containers. A plastic window box (again, with drainage holes) will do quite well, as will even a sturdy wooden crate. English gardeners are fond of using old stone troughs for this purpose, but the supply having run low even in a nation far more venerable than our own, handsome troughs are now made of tufa, a limestone rock whose alkalinity provides a beneficial influence upon the soil and a pleasingly craggy background for the plants.

Closely related to the rock container is the rock garden, where many gardeners even without any special interest in succulents have grown at least a clump of hen-and-chickens without being aware that many other hardy succulents, particularly several handsome varieties of sedum, are available. These plants are not only as easy to grow as hen-and-chickens but they are capable of providing both flowers and foliage in a wide range of colors.

All hardy succulents will thrive in a fast-draining rock garden. If your yard possesses a slope that is naturally strewn with stones and has until now been a deterrent to your gardening efforts, you have a perfect starting point. One New Jersey gardener, who built a cantilevered house on a rocky hillside that his more conventionally housed neighbors thought suitable only for mountain goats, is now envied by one and all because he has, in addition to a panoramic view, a spectacular rock garden and no lawn to mow.

If you have not been so favored by nature, choose a spot where your rock garden will blend into the topography of your land. Where possible, the garden should not have a rigid form but should be free-flowing, with borders that will appear to have been there all along.

Dig the site to a depth of about 6 inches and strew it convincingly with chunks of rubble, rock, broken brick or any other similar material. Scatter gravel loosely over chinks in the rubble and pour a mixture of 1 part topsoil, 2 parts sand and 1 part leaf mold or humus over this foundation. The exact height of the soil you add will depend on the contours of your garden, but it should always be added slowly, tamped firmly after each sizable addition (particularly along the edges) and watered gently as it is built up. Allow the soil in the rock garden to settle for a week or so before you plant in it.

Northern gardeners have a choice of dozens of hardy sempervivums and sedums, or stonecrops, to plant in their completed rock

AN UNDESERVED REPUTATION

Though the ability of the barrel cactus to store water for long periods of time makes it a favorite with gardeners who may miss a turn or two with the watering can, its reputation as a reservoir of clear, drinkable water is undeserved. If you cut off the top of a barrel cactus, you will find it filled not with water but with pulp that holds moisture like a sponge. When squeezed, the pulp yields a thick, bitter liquid. When it is cubed and boiled in sugar syrup, however, the pulp makes a pleasant dessert that tastes something like watermelon preserves and is responsible for one of the barrel cactus' other nicknames: the candy cactus.

gardens. Among the most ornamental are the evergreen *Sedum sexangulare,* whose leaves turn coppery in winter, and the *Sedum spectabile,* a large pink-flowered species that sheds its leaves in cold weather. Warm-climate gardeners, of course, have a far wider selection, since they can use tender species such as the sprawling yellow-flowered Oaxaca sedum of Mexico.

Rock gardens need not be limited to succulents, which can generally grow congenially with other plants, sharing their soil and climate requirements. Species tulips and other small-bulb plants make happy flowering companions for succulents in rock gardens, and thyme (in the north) and marjoram (in milder regions) make decorative and fragrant bedfellows in the garden as well as delicious additions to your kitchen spice rack.

A LIGHTWEIGHT PLANTER

1. *To make a lightweight outdoor planter for succulents that seems to be carved of stone, first invert one or more flowerpots in a shallow box and pack damp sand around them to form a flat-topped mound. Shape a narrow moat around the perimeter. Drape a sheet of plastic film over the sand. Cut and shape a piece of chicken wire with 1-inch mesh to match the shape of the mound, then set the wire aside. Mix 1½ parts dry peat moss, 1½ parts perlite or vermiculite and 1 part portland cement; add water gradually until the mix has the consistency of cottage cheese. Spread a 1-inch layer over the mound, then press the reinforcing chicken wire into it.*

2. *Cover the wire with another 1-inch layer, spread firmly to eliminate air pockets. Insert three or four ¾-inch wooden dowels (top) to form drainage holes.*

3. *Let the planter dry for 24 hours, then rub the top surface with a stiff-bristled brush to give it more texture. Remove the dowels. After 24 more hours of drying, invert the planter. Fill it with water, let it soak, and empty it repeatedly for several weeks before planting.*

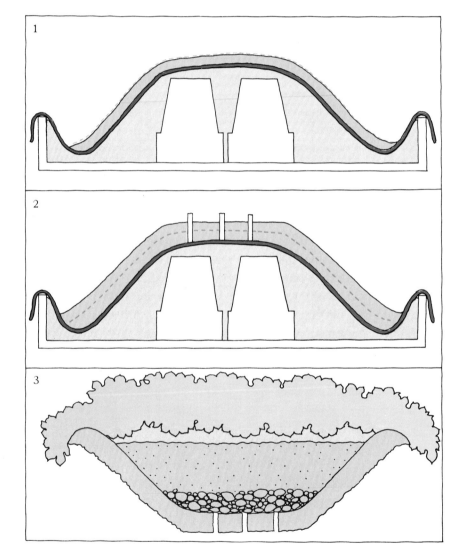

Watering in the mixed rock garden should be a bit more frequent than for the purely succulent collection, perhaps weekly in midsummer. Fertilizers in the rock garden can be a mixed blessing; most alpine plants do not need it, and it actually encourages soft leaf growth in some species. However, a scant handful of bone meal scattered over each square yard of the rockery monthly from early spring through late summer can be used to stimulate flowering.

IRON IN THE DIET

Succulents growing out of doors are relatively disease-free, but if pests become a problem they can be treated just as they are on plants growing indoors *(page 36)*. Something that is almost certain to become a problem in desert regions, and may occur in others as well, is an abnormal yellowing of the plants caused by a lack of iron. The condition is blamed on everything from poor drainage to an excess of lime in the soil, but since this malaise yields to applications of iron sulfate or iron chelate, it is not an insurmountable problem if control is begun as soon as the condition is observed. Apply the iron compounds in dilute liquid form, then repeat the treatment once a year in the spring.

In contrast to the difficulties faced by succulent growers in the rest of the nation, who must to some degree restructure their soils and then carefully select the plants to be grown in them, Southwestern gardeners have only to take advantage of generally existing land conditions and to choose their succulents from an embarrassment of riches. The ideal garden anywhere in the world looks as though its planner had refined and condensed the very best of what was available locally, and the same is true of the desert garden, which in its highest form is an inevitable extension of the nature that adjoins it. If your space is limited to the small plot typical of the suburban development house, there are several species that you can grow without eliminating such amenities as vegetable gardens and lawns. For example, Joseph's-coat cactus, a species of prickly pear, has pads streaked with pink and white and requires little space to flourish. Another possibility, the beavertail, is a bushy, low-growing prickly pear that freely produces purple flowers. The golden barrel, which is really green but is covered with golden spines, would also be a suitable choice since it attains a height of 4 feet quite slowly and will provide a dazzling springtime display of yellow flowers.

SUCCULENT GROUND COVERS

Two species of ice plant, the trailing white and the red spike, provide excellent ground cover for dry regions. These are two of the most easily available members of this large and useful group. Both plants are easy-care perennials that require little watering even in warm weather, and they bear some of the attractive blossoms they are named for almost all year long.

There is no fiat that limits a desert garden to cacti and other succulents, and a drought-resistant but nonsucculent plant such as the Spanish bayonet yucca, which slowly attains a height of 10 feet, will beautify your summers with its large white flowers. Despite its equally homicidal name, the Spanish dagger, another yucca that grows to about the same size, has soft leaf ends unlike the sharp tips found on the leaves of the Spanish bayonet and many other yuccas.

If you are blessed with a garden of ample proportions, you can use such potentially monstrous cacti as organ pipes and saguaros to accent groupings of smaller plants; if you have limited space, such semisucculent dry-area plants as beaucarneas can provide powerful accents with their thick trunks and downward-thrusting leaves, even though they do not exceed 10 feet in height. *Beaucarnea recurvata,* for example, resembles, with only minimal help from your imagination, a hoop-skirted lady wielding a feather duster in each of her several hands.

PLANTING OUTDOORS   For succulents that are to be planted in the ground, dig holes the size of their nursery containers and at the same depth, fill in around the container soil with a fresh mixture. Pack the new soil firmly around the plants and water only enough to dampen it. Heavier watering can wait until the plants have reestablished themselves, a month or so in the case of cacti. After that, a watering schedule of once a week should suffice, even in summer. Other succulents can be watered several times weekly in hot weather, and just a week or so after they have been planted. To avoid discoloration and spotting, always apply water to the soil, not to the plant, though an occasional gentle spray may be beneficial (no more than once a month) to remove pests and dirt. Neither misting nor heavy watering should occur during those parts of the day when there are extremes of temperature or sunshine.

The best time for planting a desert garden is early spring, when, as elsewhere in the world, the renewing surge of life encourages succulents to put forth their best efforts in their new home, and before the debilitating heat of the summer arrives to slow them down. If for some reason you must wait, plant in early fall, when it has cooled somewhat and the plants still have time to reestablish themselves before going into dormancy.

APPLYING FERTILIZER   If the desert garden is to bloom to the riotous degree of which it is capable, it must be encouraged by the monthly application of a phosphorus-rich (and potash-and-nitrogen-middling) fertilizer such as 15-30-15 from April to September. A solution of 1 tablespoon of fertilizer per gallon of water, applied freely to the base of each plant, is a good rule of thumb unless more specific directions are provided with the fertilizer. Withhold nourishment and cut back drastically on watering during the winter so your succulent plants will go into dormancy. The only need for watering at all in the depths of winter is to ensure that the roots do not die back completely before the resumption of active growth.

Certain succulents, such as echeverias and aeoniums, also require a careful regimen of pruning. In the case of many species, pruning becomes a matter of life and death, rather than merely an effort to keep the garden reasonably neat. For instance, *Aeonium tabulaeforme,* a stemless species, produces a handsome solitary rosette 18 inches in diameter. Once it reaches mature size, the center converts into a flowering spike of stately yellow flowers, then the plant dies. So long as buds are pruned off and flowering is prevented, death is postponed. However, leaf cuttings taken from young plants will bloom within two or three years, so it is possible to enjoy the flowers of mature plants and have a supply of young plants coming along to replace them.

Gardeners who grow hardy succulents face a similar dilemma with sempervivums, some of which have the same propensity toward death after bloom. Since they can be effortlessly propagated from cuttings—as can branching varieties of aeoniums and echeverias— you can easily grow duplicates of any whose generosity in flowering for you becomes their final offering.

Succulent gardens can, unfortunately, become as weed choked as conventional plantings, and while the result may not be fatal, weeds can set back the growth of the garden considerably besides marring its beauty. In warmer regions of the country, weeding is a year-long chore, especially in desert areas, where winter rains bring on wave after wave of weeds, even in January. In addition, desert gardeners must battle such far-ranging interlopers as tumbleweed, mournfully praised in cowboy ballads but cursed by Southwest gardeners because the top of the plant becomes detached from its roots in autumn and is driven by the wind about the countryside, scattering seeds as it goes.

AND ALWAYS THE WEEDS

For the dry-climate gardener, the tumbleweed is only a small manifestation of the maintenance needed to prevent a carefully created succulent garden from reverting to a totally unkempt natural state. The cold- and the wet-climate succulent gardeners are faced with the reverse of this problem: their energies must be directed to ensuring the survival and continued health of the species chosen, for despite their hardiness, some of them may adjust only with great difficulty to the demands made on them. In either case, the pleasure produced by rising to the challenge is sure to outweigh the pains.

Succulents for all seasons and settings

That cacti and other succulents can be grown readily indoors is no surprise, but that some of the same plants can be cultivated outdoors in virtually all parts of the country—not just the Southwest—astonishes many gardeners. The fact is that there are species that thrive outdoors not only in the subtropical Gulf Coast states and the damp Northwest but even in the subzero temperatures and blanketing snow of the Northeast.

To be sure, a spectacular outdoor cactus and succulent garden is not simple to create, even where the climate is ideal. "You're very much mistaken if you think it's easy," says the gardener blessed with the mild, dry climate of the Southern California garden on the opposite page. "The whole thing will become a jungle if the succulents are not constantly thinned and pruned." With a half-acre garden to maintain, at least she does not need to worry about soil conditions. But planting an outdoor succulent garden in regions other than the natural cactus country of the Southwest generally requires careful preparation of the soil to assure fast drainage, since succulents often rot in wet ground. Unless you happen to have a rocky or hilly area at hand, you may need to construct an artificial slope for drainage *(page 55)*.

The better the soil conditions you can offer cacti and succulents, the greater your chances will be of ensuring their survival despite such unfavorable conditions as high humidity, heavy rains or the withering blasts of Northern winters. Keeping soil on the dry side, however, is not enough; just as important is an informed selection of species of succulents that are strong enough to withstand the vagaries of weather in your region. Often you will simply have to experiment, as did the Long Island gardener who designed the circular bed of cacti and succulents on pages 68-69, to discover which plants will adapt best to your garden environment. But the effort will be worthwhile. All of the gardens shown here have endured years in the open, and are living proof of the wide-ranging possibilities of outdoor succulent cultivation.

Boasting more than 200 species of cacti and succulents, a lush garden near San Diego gives a closely clipped lawn the magical aura of a clearing in the wilderness.

At home on the range

In the dry heat of the desert sun, where afternoon temperatures often climb well above 100° and shade and rainfall are rare commodities, the hardiest plants must struggle to survive. But drought-defying cacti and succulents enable Southwestern gardeners to turn the desert to their advantage, mirroring its native plant life in gardens where the naturally sandy soil offers a perfect setting for ocotillos, opuntias, aloes and other cacti and succulents.

Planted in orderly fashion astride a gravel pathway, desert-dwelling cacti and succulents—including the 4-foot-high sculptural agaves in the foreground—bring the wide expanse of surrounding wilderness into a Tucson, Arizona, garden. The plants are watered weekly the year round.

Old-man cactus in Florida

The sight of an old-man cactus hoisting its hoary head from chalky coral in a Florida garden, framed by swaying palm-tree fronds, is enough to make a gardener suspect he has succumbed to sunstroke. But dazzling displays of cacti and succulents can be grown in the subtropical Southeast, despite high humidity. A coral base provides excellent drainage, and weekly weeding and fungicide sprayings help minimize the damp climate's adverse effects.

In striking contrast to the verdant, palmy background, a naturally bleached grouping of stout old-man cacti bedded in stark-white coral calls attention to a Florida succulent garden. The bed also harbors barrel cacti, mammillarias, a flowering crown-of-thorns—and a weathered cow skull.

Snow or no, north they go

Peeking from beneath a blanket of snow, hardy cacti and succulents, ensconced in outdoor gardens in such surprising places as New York, Wisconsin and the Dakotas, have proved they can survive almost anywhere. The frost and wetness of northern winters are formidable problems, but as long as the gardener provides quick-draining soil and clears away choking weeds, some opuntias, agaves, coryphanthas and pediocacti are likely to endure.

Robust and blossoming in early summer, dormant and snow-covered in winter (inset), hardy cacti and succulents brave the highly variable northern climate of a bed 15 feet wide near the shore of Long Island Sound. Encouraged by the sandy soil, most of these plants have survived several years in the open.

A carpet for cloud country

Normally found clinging to rocky mountainsides 4,000 to 5,000 feet above sea level, alpine succulents such as sedums and sempervivums can turn cool, moist Northwestern gardens into richly textured carpets of color. Easily grown in almost any well-drained area, they will withstand temperatures ranging from below zero to above 100°. With commendable restraint, the gardener whose succulents are shown below remarks, "They are constantly surprising."

Hardy sedums and sempervivums cover not only the lava-rock bed of an Oregon garden but the roof of a shed as well. In Europe, sempervivums on the roof were once believed to ward off lightning and the devil; in this case, the gardener simply tossed succulents onto the roof where they rooted in the moss.

To multiply the brood: seed and surgery 4

Succulents are so prodigal in their reproductive habits that anyone who is at all interested in them can propagate a sizable collection quickly and easily. Succulents can be grown from seed, raised from various types of cuttings and, in the case of the cactus family, produced by grafting one plant onto another.

Succulent seed, most of which is exceedingly small, has an extremely high rate of germination but is not recommended for those gardeners who demand instant gratification, since a wait of a year or longer for a recognizable plant is not uncommon. If you do not have the patience to wait around for sprouts to become identifiable, succulents provide two alternatives: ordinary cuttings, which root more successfully than do those of any other group of plants; and offsets, which are miniatures growing upon the parent, sometimes fully rooted and simply waiting to be gently plucked away and started on lives of their own.

The art of grafting can produce equally fast results, sometimes instantaneous enough to satisfy a magician. Furthermore, of all the possible ways to get new plants, grafting is surely the most fascinating, conveying as it does upon its practitioner the possibility of playing Dr. Frankenstein and creating even more fantastic shapes in a family already liberally supplied with them by nature. Except for euphorbias, most other succulents do not lend themselves to grafting as do cacti, since they lack the inner ring of nutrient-carrying vascular channels that make the process possible.

In discriminating hands, grafting can result in such popular oddities as the ubiquitous moon cactus, which consists of a gymnocalycium scion, the rootless upper portion, grafted onto a hylocereus stock, the rooted parent plant. The vivid red and orange colors of the scion are not dyed, as is widely thought, but are the result of continuous selection and hybridizing. Unfortunately, these flamboyant cacti have also had all of the green chlorophyll bred out of them,

Tucked neatly into wooden flats, these one-and two-year-old sempervivums are ready to be planted outdoors. They are easily propagated by rooting the tiny offsets, which are known as chicks.

so they must be grafted to vigorous stocks just to remain alive. The scions, which are raised from seeds, are grafted at the age of three weeks; those you buy at a plant store are about seven months old. The offsets that eventually form around their bases cannot be rooted like those of other types of cacti but must also be grafted to life-sustaining stocks.

THE GRAFT RATIONALE

The same grafting process used in producing the moon cactus is an invaluable tool for all serious cactus growers, for it enables them to bring seedlings to maturity far more quickly than they otherwise could, an especially valuable process with new hybrids. Grafting can also save a plant that otherwise would die; a viable portion, perhaps significantly less than half of the plant, can be mounted upon a robust stock and thus brought back to health. When the scion has recuperated and in addition produced some of the vigorous growth common in such cases, it can be cut from the stock, rooted in sand and perlite like any other cutting, and returned to a pot of its own. When separating what in effect is a temporary graft, care should be taken to leave a small part of the scion attached to the stock: it will produce offsets that can be rooted and potted separately, so the process will not only save the life of the scion but increase its numbers at the same time.

Another application of grafting is the placement of naturally trailing species such as Christmas cactus and epiphyllums upon trunks that elevate them, just as one does in the creation of tree roses, so the sweeping branches are better displayed. Growers often graft cactus plants simply because they are dissatisfied with existing roots and stems and feel that they are too undeveloped to support the rest of the plants.

Some experts hold the opinion that any cactus can be grafted to any other, while others feel that participants in cactus unions, unlike those in human ones, should be closely related to produce the best results. In either event, the stock, which is slated to bear the eventual load, must be sturdy enough to handle the job. The professional rule of thumb is that the stock must weigh an astonishing 10 times as much as the scion.

SPRING, WHEN SAP RISES

The best time of year for grafting is, as you might expect, early spring, when the sap of cacti and almost everything else is rising. But there are a few exceptions: ideally Christmas cacti, which are winter blooming, would be grafted onto stocks which share their schedule, with their south-of-the-equator juices flowing in late fall.

There are four commonly employed techniques in grafting: flat, cleft, stab and side. Most frequently used is the flat graft, the easiest and the most suitable for most operations. Regardless of the type of graft you undertake, use a stainless-steel knife; some cacti will turn ordinary steel black.

To start a flat graft, simply slice the top from the stock at a point where it will be wide enough to accommodate the base of the scion. The cut should be made where the stem feels firm, not soft and watery as it would be near the growing tip. Then remove a segment of the scion, and join the two for a trial fitting to make sure the visible ring of vascular tissue on each part matches reasonably well. You may need to cut away the spines and the tops of the protruding ribs on the stock and scion. When the two halves are ready to be joined, cut a transparently thin slice from the previously prepared end of each partner, discard the slices and press the two parts together gently but firmly to force out any air bubbles. The sap on the original cuts will have begun to dry in the brief time taken for trial fitting, and since the success of the graft depends upon fusion in the partner plants, get it off to a fresh running start. Be sure the vascular rings are as closely aligned as possible to ensure optimum conditions for the graft.

Since it will take several weeks to complete an effective graft, the two halves must be held together artificially. One way to do this with small cacti is to pass two rubber bands at right angles to each other over the top of the scion and the bottom of the pot; the bands will not only hold the two halves together but will expand to accommodate the growth that will be taking place. With larger cacti, simply drape strings weighted with hardware nuts over the top to hold the parts together. Remove rubber bands or strings when a slight pressure of your fingers at the point of the graft produces no movement in the scion.

When the scion is flat and almost two-dimensional in comparison with other forms of cacti, the cleft graft, in which the scion is inserted in the stock rather than seated upon it, is used. The Christmas cactus is often grafted by this method. Detach the scion from the plant at a joint, taper the end into the shape of an arrowhead and insert it into a corresponding slot in the top of the stock. A cactus spine such as that of an opuntia is the ideal material for securing the graft, since it can be left to self-destruct in the new plant leaving barely a trace. If you do not have a cactus spine handy, use a toothpick. It must eventually be removed but leaves no aftereffects except small scars.

An alternative to the cleft graft is the stab graft, in which the base of the scion of a trailing species is sharpened to a wedge and thrust into a prepared incision in the stock, generally a flat and otherwise unaltered pad such as that of the opuntia.

BINDING THE WOUNDS

75

Long, slender scions, such as those of the peanut cactus, are usually side-grafted to their stocks. In a side graft, the meeting points of scion and stock are cut diagonally; when the two are joined, the upward direction of the lower surface provides a wider support for the elongated scion. A side graft is pinned together with spines or toothpicks, then tied together with a length of string or raffia until the joint is solid enough so they can be removed.

Newly grafted cacti should be kept in a shaded place but only until their wounds have healed. If the grafting is being done on an outdoor plant, protect it from the sun by placing a paper bag over it until any exposed cut edge has dried. Water the grafted cactus on the same schedule as other cacti *(page 35),* but do not wet the grafting point itself, since any moisture that lodges in it may promote rot and invite pests. With reasonable care catastrophes can be avoided. When all the supportive paraphernalia are removed, the new plants can join your collection and be treated in the same manner as the senior members.

THE SIMPLICITY OF SEEDS
After the intricacies of grafting cacti, growing them and the other succulents from seed will seem comparatively simple. Most home propagators will be working with fresh seeds bought in packets. That is an easy way to acquire species you do not already have and perhaps could not buy as plants. Since probably half of all cacti do not bloom in cultivation, your own seed selection will be meager at best, unless you are fortunate enough to live in an area where cacti proliferate naturally.

Still, if you are fortunate enough to have a ripe seed pod about to burst open on one of your succulents (and it can be quite a burst: the common crassula can release up to a thousand seeds from one tiny pod) you should certainly try to grow them; plants raised from seeds are generally healthier, more perfectly formed and more easily acclimated than those propagated in other ways. A dark color on a seed is a reliable indicator of ripeness. Some succulent seeds, particularly those of epiphyllums, will be encased in gummy matter even when they are ripe, and this must be removed by wrapping the mess in cheesecloth and washing it with running water. The seeds that remain should be dried on a paper towel before they are planted. Most succulent seeds require no other preparation, but the seeds of some of the larger opuntia species and some others are encased in hard shells that must be soaked and notched, just as are those of the less exotic morning glory.

Almost anything that comes to hand, provided it is scrupulously clean, can be used as a container for sowing the seed. An old clay pot will serve, as will a porous tray or a discarded but only slightly leaking cooking utensil. Sterilize the container chosen with boiling water. Fill it one-third full with gravel, then to just below the rim with a cactus soil mixture *(page 34)* that does not contain any large lumps. The mix should not be excessively fine, since a homogenized planting medium will, when it is watered, tend to compress and confine the seedlings and sprouts, thus inhibiting their development. Soak the soil before you plant in it by setting the container almost to its own depth in tepid water until the soil is thoroughly moistened, then remove it and allow it to drain briefly.

The seed should be evenly scattered over the surface of the mixture and covered with a very thin sprinkling of fine sand. Cover the seed container with a sheet of glass or plastic to prevent rapid evaporation of moisture. A glass cover should be tinted so that the sun's warmth reaches the seeds without roasting them; if plastic is used, it should be opaque rather than clear. If clear glass is used, move it to provide a small opening during the warmest part of the day so the seeds are not injured. Some condensation should always be present on the underside of the cover. If it is sparse, moisten the soil immediately and from the bottom only; if heavy droplets of condensation form, wipe the glass until it is dry. But it is crucial that the soil be kept barely damp at all times.

A MOIST, WARM BED

The brilliant red of these cactus fruit, borne by a Melocactus obtusipetalus, serves as a beacon to lure birds, insects and rodents that will help ensure the survival of this species. One ripe fruit (right) has been bitten by a field mouse, exposing tiny black seeds. Some of the seeds will pass through the mouse's digestive tract. When they later sprout, the new plants will be scattered widely enough so that they will not compete with the parent plant for scarce moisture.

Seeds germinate best at a temperature of about 80° both day and night. In a warm room with a sunny window sill the seeds may sprout without supplemental heat, but you can eliminate the gamble with thermostatically regulated soil-heating cables or pads, available at some garden centers and by mail through seed catalogues. They provide what is called bottom heat because it originates beneath the soil in a seed flat or in the gravel drainage bed beneath seed pots. The early part of the summer is the safest time for propagation, since by then there is little danger that a cold night could become a lethal problem.

Some visible signs of growth should appear within three weeks unless you have chosen a rare genus such as *Parodia,* which may take up to a year to germinate. Since it is important for the seedlings to have some fresh air, push the glass or plastic covering of the container back a bit more each day, starting with perhaps an inch, and in a few weeks removing it entirely. Too much air and light all at once may discolor or burn the seedlings, and it is important that soil be kept moist while the seedlings are hardened for exposure to open air. The seedlings should remain in the pots until the following spring unless they grow so rapidly that they crowd one another, in which case they must be thinned immediately.

TENDER IS THE MOVE   Succulent seedlings should be removed carefully, even tenderly. For this purpose, a notched tack remover or a nicked ice-cream stick is useful. Prepare a hole large enough to receive the roots of the transplant in either a less crowded corner of the same container or in a freshly prepared one. Firm the seedling lightly in place, moisten the soil to remove air pockets, then care for the transplant as though it had never been uprooted at all. It will take about six months for most succulents to become large enough to handle; the giant saguaro may be only ¼ inch tall after two years. Then the plants should be given more space in containers filled with a soil mixture consisting of 2 parts sand, 1 part leaf mold and 1 part potting soil. As soon as the young succulents have attained enough size, pot them individually *(opposite).*

If you find the slow growth of seedlings too agonizing to endure, cuttings are second only to grafts in the speed with which they provide their admirers with new plants. A succulent cutting, taken from a leaf or from a stem that has several leaf nodes, can strike enough roots to enable it to stand on its own within three weeks. Root the cuttings in containers filled with a half-and-half mixture of sand and perlite. This should be dampened but not soaked, since the cuttings to be placed in it will be rootless and not only will be unable to utilize excessive water but may be rotted by it.

Cuttings should be taken in the spring when they are ready to make their strongest growth and when they may expect the longest possible growing period before winter forces them into dormancy. Though cuttings do not require as much warmth as seeds do, they do need a temperature of about 70°, so propagate them only when the weather is beginning to warm. If you cannot wait for spring, you can use electric cables to warm the soil.

Cuttings may be taken from any part of the plant, but it is best to remove them at a natural separation point such as a joint, so their absence does not affect the appearance of a treasured specimen. Columnar cacti such as the cerei are sad exceptions, since they must be subjected to a form of scalping—a sizable segment must be removed below the tip. This does not kill the cactus, but actually stimulates new growth below the truncated area. In taking a cutting from the top of a plant growing outdoors, be careful to make a diagonal cut so rain will not accumulate on the wound. Dust the wound with powdered fungicide or charcoal to prevent rot. Once removed from the parent plant, the cutting should rest in a shaded place from several days to a week or more for larger cuttings until the wound feels dry and healed, or callused.

If the cutting is a long leaf, as in the aloe, gasteria, haworthia or sansevieria, it is not necessary to use the leaf in its entirety; it can be

SEED AS THE SOURCE

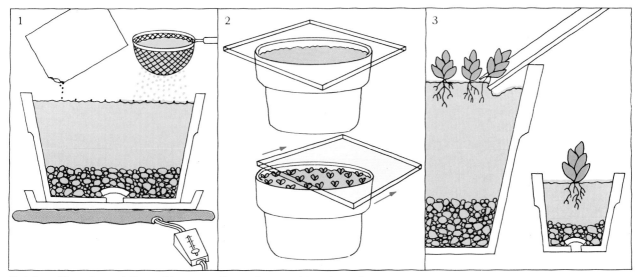

Put gravel in a clay pot, then add a mix of 1 part potting soil and 2 parts sharp sand. Dampen from the bottom. Scatter succulent seeds and cover them lightly with sifted sand. Put a heat pad under the pot at night.

Cover the pot with a piece of glass and place it in a warm, sunny spot. On hot days, slide the glass open slightly to avoid roasting the seed. When seedlings appear, slide the cover off gradually to acclimate them to open air.

When seedlings are about an inch high or are crowding their pot, pick them out with a forked stick and transplant them to 3-inch pots. Moisten the soil immediately to remove air pockets around the roots.

snipped into 3- to 4-inch segments to make several plants. As with any succulent cutting, let calluses form on the cut ends. Then press each piece into a cutting bed (below), making sure the base end of each segment is at the bottom.

Perhaps the most unusual technique of propagating cuttings is utilized with the green fruit of an opuntia cactus. If you lay such a fruit on its side in a cutting bed and press it down only slightly, it will root in about three weeks, and a recognizable opuntia pad will emerge from the fruit in just a few months, providing you with an unusual example of green fruit regeneration.

Some succulents do not even wait for their leaves to be removed by the grower: the Boston bean sedum, so named for its plump russet leaves, drops some of them during the course of the summer and is soon surrounded by other Boston bean sedums. Anyone who has ever grown the kalanchoe plant called variously "mother of hundreds" or "mother of thousands" is familiar with its similarly invasive propensities; it drops the plantlets that grow along the edges of its leaves into the pots of adjacent plants and may smother them by sheer force of numbers.

The healed cuttings will root best if they can be made to stand shallowly in the cutting bed. If they fall over, bind them to tooth-picks with plant ties and push the tips of the picks into the bed. Though cuttings need warmth, they should not be in direct sunlight; place them in a lightly shaded area. Keep the bed barely moist until roots are formed. If natural light is insufficient, cuttings will root and seedlings will germinate under the cool light of fluorescent lamps. A

QUICK START WITH CUTTINGS

Succulent cuttings taken from a parent plant (top row) and planted in sharp sand or a mixture of half sand and half perlite (bottom row) often produce recognizable plants in a few months. Choose large, plump segments, letting them dry and callus before planting. Most cuttings will callus over the cut in a few days; a large cutting may take up to 10 days. Set cuttings in the soil just deep enough to stand alone. Tie a tall cutting to a stake for support (lower right). Put cuttings in a warm, shady spot and keep the soil barely moist. When roots have formed, repot in a mix of 1 part potting soil to 1 part sharp sand.

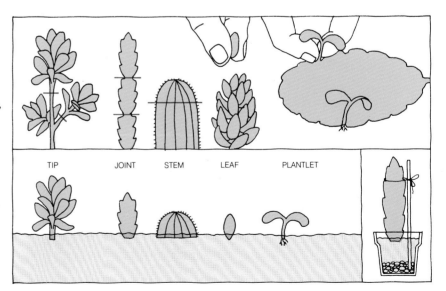

TIP   JOINT   STEM   LEAF   PLANTLET

two-tube, 20-watt fixture turned on for 16 hours a day can handle 35 to 50 cuttings at a time. To germinate seeds, place the top of the seedbed within 6 inches of such a fixture, and maintain a temperature of 70° to 75°.

Most cuttings will be rooted during a month's time. Test them by tugging at them gently; if they do not yield easily, they are probably ready to be potted individually. If they prove not to be well rooted, they can always be put back into the bed.

Favorites such as the hen-and-chickens have yet another claim upon the succulent grower's affections: they need not be grown from seed or even rooted from cuttings. They can be divided into already-rooted clumps simply by cutting the chicks away from the hen and planting them to raise their own broods. This method of propagation can be used for any of the succulents that share the mat-forming habits of the hen-and-chickens, such as the echeverias and the dudleyas. Though offsets such as the chicks are common, they are not always ready to stand on their own; these must be cleanly cut away from the parent plant and rooted as are any other cuttings.

If you are a neophyte only recently converted to the exciting avocation of propagating cacti and succulents, you may be startled by their fecundity. In fact, you may be as overwhelmed as a successful novice vegetable gardener at the peak of his harvest. The fruits of your labors may well overflow the space you had originally planned to devote to them, and you will be imploring all your visitors to take them home by the armful. This is the kind of dilemma that any dedicated gardener is delighted to live with.

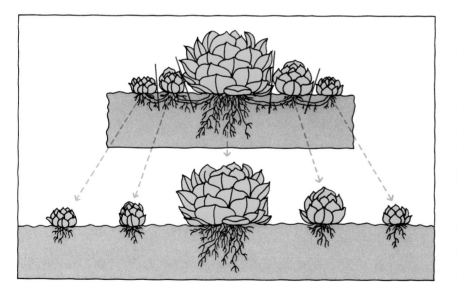

INSTANT START WITH OFFSETS

Many succulents can be propagated from offsets, which are plantlets—often with their own root systems—that are connected by underground lateral stems to the parent plants. To separate a single offset, expose the lateral stem and sever it with a sharp knife. Remove the offset and place it in the shade until the part of the stem that has been cut dries out and forms a callus, then replant it. Also let the cut stem of the parent plant callus before you cover it with soil. To propagate several offsets at once, dig up the parent plant, separate the offsets and let the wounds callus before replanting parent and offsets.

The creative craft of grafting

Grafting, the joining of a piece of stem from one cactus to a cut in the rooted stem of another, opens up a bewitching world for the cactus gardener. It can be used to rescue a weak or dying plant or to speed up, sometimes by as much as a year or two, the growth of seedlings to the flowering stage. It can also provide a pendant plant, such as a Christmas cactus, with a pedestal for its trailing stems.

But more than this, grafting offers the gardener the fun of producing new plants not found anywhere in nature. It is even possible to graft many different kinds of cacti onto one supporting plant.

Cacti and some succulent euphorbias lend themselves to grafting more readily than other plants, for each plant has an inner ring of vascular tissue that can be easily seen and matched to another plant's ring. A careful match is essential in promoting a free flow of nutritious sap from the rooted parent plant, called the stock, to the grafted-on section, called the scion. The best time to do grafting is in the spring when a new period of growth is just beginning. Choose a stock that is well rooted and juicy and a scion taken from a firm and healthy growing tip of a new offshoot. In most instances the scion should be the same diameter as the stock or smaller.

Make all cuts with a sharp knife sterilized in denatured alcohol. Join the plants quickly with slight pressure to force out air bubbles that might cause cut surfaces to dry. Secure with weighted strings, rubber bands stretched over and under the graft, toothpicks or the spines from any cactus, depending on the method of grafting used. (Details of four grafting methods are shown on the pages that follow.) Spines make the best anchors because they can remain inside the plant and leave but slight scars.

Keep grafted plants dry and out of direct sun for two to four weeks until the scion does not move when it is pressed lightly—an indication that the graft has begun to grow together. If your main objective is to regenerate the scion, wait until it shows vigorous growth, which might be as long as a year or two, then cut it off the stock and root it in sand to stand alone once more.

A stranger in the already strange land of cacti, this gnomish woolly-headed plant was created by grafting an old-lady cactus scion atop a Peruvian apple cactus stock.

Step-by-step to a new plant

There are four basic methods used to graft cacti, each named according to the way they are cut: flat, in which scion and stock are cut straight across and then joined; side, in which stock and scion are cut at 45° angles and then joined; cleft, in which a wedge-shaped scion is fitted into a cleft in the stock; and stab, in which the scion is wedged into a deep stab in the stock. The seedling graft (*opposite*) is a variation of the flat graft; it is used to speed growth.

THE FLAT GRAFT

Thick, round scions, like the three-year-old mammillaria astride the column cactus at left, commonly call for the use of a flat graft. It is the simplest graft because matching a good portion of the inner vascular rings in each piece is relatively easy with flat surfaces. To make a flat graft, slice off a healthy scion of a diameter to match the stock, then bevel the cut end slightly (left). Remove the top of the stock and bevel the edge downward so stock and scion will stay snugly together (below, left). When both pieces are ready, remove a final thin slice from each part. Press the pieces together with rings carefully matched. Drape strings weighted with hardware nuts over the scion (below, right). Keep the plant dry and out of direct sun until the parts begin to grow together, then remove the strings.

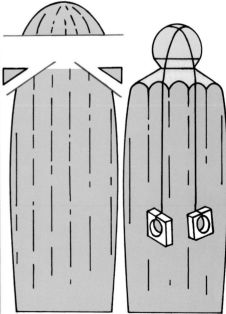

SCION: MAMMILLARIA PROLIFERA
STOCK: ACANTHOCEREUS PENTAGONUS

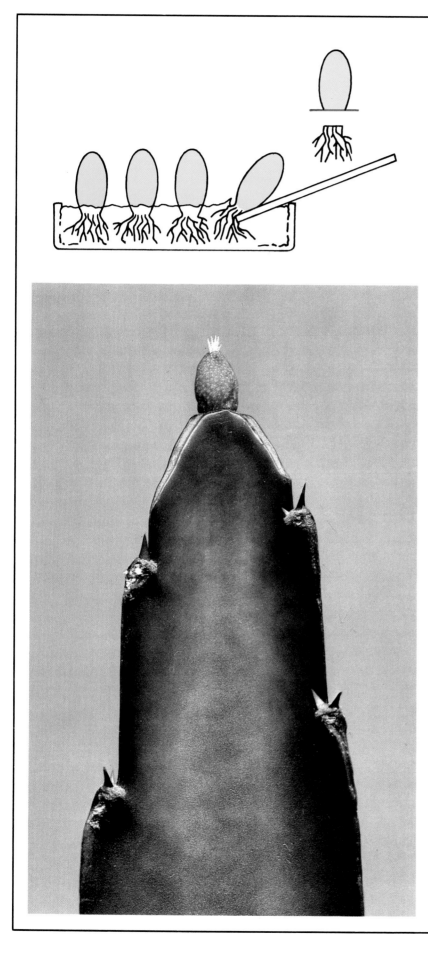

THE SEEDLING GRAFT

The tiny seedling perched atop the nursing stock at left will mature several times faster than if it had been left growing on its own. To graft a seedling, remove the top of the stock plant; bevel the cut edge only if spines would interfere with the graft (below, top). Pry the seedling out of its container with a pencil or plant marker and slice off the roots (left). Take a final thin slice from the cut end of the stock and join the two plants, making sure the base of the seedling touches the stock's vascular ring (below, bottom). The seedling does not need to be secured; it is so tiny it will stick to the moist end of the stock plant. Keep the plants out of direct sunlight until the graft takes and keep the exposed cut dry. Several seedlings can be grafted onto a single stock.

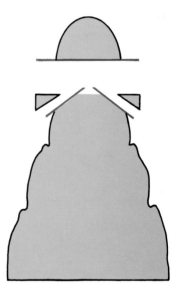

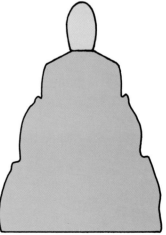

SCION: MAMMILLARIA SEEDLING
STOCK: HYLOCEREUS UNDATUS

THE SIDE GRAFT

Two slender cacti have been side-grafted to produce the single whisker-topped stalk at left. To make a side graft, cut stock and scion at matching 45° angles, then join the two quickly, making sure their inner vascular rings touch (below). Fasten with toothpicks or cactus spines; if further support is needed, bind with a soft cord. Keep out of direct sun until the joint starts to heal, usually two to four weeks, then remove the cord and toothpicks. Spines used for grafting need not be removed; they will leave only inconspicuous scars.

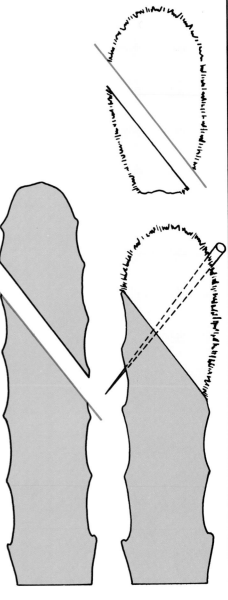

SCION: HILDWINTERIA AURIESPINA
STOCK: SELENICEREUS PTERANTHUS

THE CLEFT GRAFT

The cleft graft is commonly used for trailing scions like the Christmas cactus at left. Remove the top of the stock, then slice a cleft, ½ inch deep, into the edge. Leave the slice in place to keep the cut moist. Sever the scion at a stem joint, then taper the cut end (below, left). Remove the slice from the cleft and insert the scion so vascular rings touch. Fasten with spines or toothpicks and wrap with a soft cord (below, right). Keep dry and shaded until the graft starts to heal, then remove the cord and toothpicks.

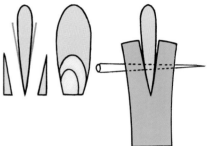

SCION: SCHLUMBERGERA TRUNCATA
STOCK: PERESKIOPSIS GATESII

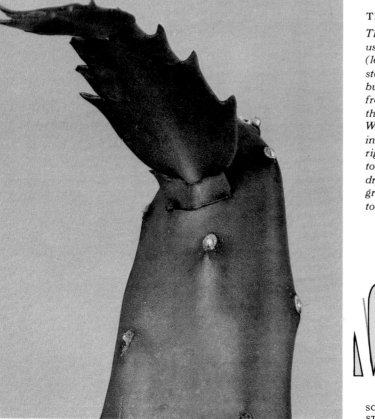

THE STAB GRAFT

The stab graft, like the cleft graft, is used primarily to elevate trailing cacti (left). Cut a deep slash into the stock plant, either upward or downward but not through it. Sever the scion from its parent plant at a stem joint, then taper the cut (below, left). Wedge the scion into the stab wound so inner vascular rings touch (below, right). If necessary, fasten with toothpicks or cactus spines. Keep dry and out of direct sunlight until the graft begins to heal, then remove the toothpicks or trim the grafting spines.

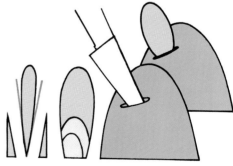

SCION: SCHLUMBERGERA TRUNCATA
STOCK: OPUNTIA MAXIMA

Pedestals for beauty

Grafted cacti have a bizarre and otherworldly beauty. Many, like the white-topped specimen below, seem treelike, mounted on long slender stalks with strange furry or bulbous branches; others are decidedly schizoid in appearance, with a split personality like that of the flowering Oriental moon cactus at right. The popularity of the moon cactus stems from the colorful gymnocalycium scions; these are not dyed, as commonly supposed, but have obtained their red and orange tint through years of hybridization. Green chlorophyll has been bred out of them; in order to survive, they must now be grafted onto a plant that retains food-making ability. The plant at lower left is not a moon cactus, however; it has a rare chlorophyll-free *Neoporteria* as a scion.

SCION: NEOPORTERIA CHILENSIS
STOCK: CEREUS PERUVIANUS

SCION: MAMMILLARIA FRAGILIS
STOCK: SELENICEREUS MACDONALDIAE

SCION: GYMNOCALYCIUM MIHANOVICHII
STOCK: HARRISIA JUSBERTII

SCION: COLEOCEPHALOCEREUS AUREUS
STOCK: CEREUS PERUVIANUS

SCION: REBUTIA HELIOSA
STOCK: HYLOCEREUS GUATAMALENSIS

An encyclopedia of cacti and succulents 5

As house plants go, cacti and succulents are about as easy to get along with as anyone could wish. The great majority originally were desert dwellers, so they thrive in the low winter humidity of a tightly built modern house that would curl the fronds of a fern overnight. These lovers of light seem to stretch forth to welcome the hot rays of the sun beating in on them. They accept with equanimity the neglect of a casual gardener who goes away for a week or so without bothering to hire a plant sitter. Some of them, in fact, are so rugged they will breeze through the rigors of a northern winter outdoors.

These remarkable plants have incredible variety, demonstrated by the more than 200 species in the encyclopedia that follows. These plants are described and their growing requirements detailed—the optimum amounts of light and water, the best kind of potting mix and fertilizer, the frost tolerance or lack thereof.

In themselves, these requirements can tell you much about the plants. If a high-phosphorus fertilizer is called for, you know that the plant needs this extra inducement in order to bloom well; a high nitrogen requirement suggests that strong vegetative growth is more critical. The need for limestone reflects the desert heritage: in that environment, scanty rainfall leaves concentrations of surface minerals that make the soil alkaline.

Cacti and succulents in the encyclopedia are listed alphabetically by internationally recognized Latin botanical names—first the genus (or general) name, then the species (or specific) name, sometimes followed by a third name, that of the variety, if that variety is exceptional. The sometimes weird and often wonderful common names by which many of these plants have come to be known— bunny ears, drunkard's dream, devil's backbone, string-of-beads, queen-of-the-night—are cross-referenced to their more precise Latin equivalents. On pages 151-153 is a quick-reference chart summarizing the characteristics of all the illustrated species.

The spectacular blooms opposite are the springtime fireworks of desert cacti. Colored foliage decorates other succulents—the gray of the silver crown (lower right) and the deep purple of the black tree (left center).

DESERT ROSE
Adenium obesum

PLOVER EGGS
Adromischus festivus

A

ADENIUM

A. obesum (desert rose)
Size: To 3 feet tall as a pot plant; 7 to 15 feet outdoors

A succulent native to eastern Africa and southern Arabia, the desert rose grows into a small tree with a knobby trunk and branches. It has oblong, fleshy leaves, 3 to 6 inches long, clustered at branch tips. The undersides of the leaves are covered with small white hairs. In early summer, 5-inch flowers appear, their five rounded petals a deep pink around the edges, fading to pale centers. The desert rose has no spines but produces a poisonous milky sap. The plants grow slowly, producing 1 to 2 inches of new growth each year.

HOW TO GROW. Outdoors, plants are hardy only in Zone 10. They need full sun and moderate humidity. Plant them in a well-drained sandy loam and feed them each spring with bone meal. Indoors, the desert rose grows best with four or more hours a day of direct sunlight or with strong artificial light for 12 hours or more a day. It will grow fairly well in bright indirect light reflected from pale walls. When they are actively growing in summer, indoor plants need 75° to 85° day temperatures and 65° to 70° night temperatures. In winter the temperatures should be 10° lower. Provide moderate to high humidity.

Use equal parts commercial potting soil and sharp sand, with 1 tablespoon of ground limestone and 1 tablespoon of bone meal added to each gallon of the mix. Allow the soil to become moderately dry between thorough waterings from spring through fall; water less often in winter. Do not fertilize newly potted or purchased plants for a year. Feed established plants once in the spring with 1 teaspoon of bone meal to a 4- to 6-inch pot. When a plant crowds its pot, transfer it in spring to a pot one size larger. Propagate from cuttings.

ADROMISCHUS

A. clavifolius (pretty pebbles); *A. festivus* (plover eggs)
Size: 1 to 3 inches tall

Native to southern Africa, succulents of the *Adromischus* genus grow wild in various habitats, from sandy soil at sea level to mountainous, rocky areas. They have thick, fleshy leaves usually tightly packed on very short stems to form clumps of chubby rosettes. The leaves vary in shape, color and texture but most have a smooth surface and usually are gray-green and plain or spotted with red or purple. Occasionally, in summer, small five-petaled flowers appear on thin stems, but the plants are chiefly valued for their foliage.

Pretty pebbles has cylindrical leaves slightly flattened and wavy at the tips. Gray-green with red speckles, the smooth leaves are 1 to 3 inches long and ½ inch wide. Half-inch flowers line 1-foot flower stalks. Plover eggs has club-shaped leaves, which are mottled with purplish or reddish brown. They measure up to 2 inches long and up to 1 inch wide. The 14-inch flower stalks rise above clustering plants, bearing small white, red or pink flowers. Indoors, grow the plants in individual shallow pots or in dish gardens; outdoors, in trough rock gardens or containers.

HOW TO GROW. These succulents grow best indoors where they get four or more hours of direct sunlight each day or 14 to 16 hours of strong artificial light. They grow fairly well in bright indirect light such as that reflected from light walls. Bright light intensifies the colors. The ideal temperatures in spring, summer and fall are 50° to 70° at night and 70° to 90° in the daytime. In winter, ideal temperatures are 45° to 55° at night and 60° to 75° in the daytime. Low to moderate humidity is preferable. From spring through fall, let the soil become moderately dry between thorough waterings. In winter, water only enough to keep plants from shriveling.

Grow in a potting mixture of 1 part commercial potting soil and 1 part sharp sand. To each gallon of the mixture, add 1 tablespoon of ground limestone and 1 tablespoon of bone meal. Feed established plants once each spring, using 1 teaspoon of bone meal to a 4- to 6-inch pot, or use a foliage-house-plant fertilizer, such as 10-20-10, diluted to half the minimum strength recommended on the label. Do not feed newly established plants the first year. Repot overcrowded plants in the spring. Propagate from seeds, leaf cuttings or stem cuttings in the spring or summer.

Outdoors, the plants are hardy only in Zone 10. Plants require full sun or lightly filtered sunlight and a dry atmosphere. Plant in well-drained sandy loam. Work ground limestone and bone meal into the soil before planting.

AEONIUM
A. arboreum atropurpureum (black tree); *A. haworthii* (pin wheel)
Size: 10 inches to 3 feet tall

These highly adaptable succulents, native to northern Africa, Madeira and the Canary Islands, grow from sea level to 6,000 feet. At one time considered to be sempervivums, they form small shrubs with symmetrical rosettes of flattened leaves at the ends of woody stems and branches. In late winter or early spring, mature stems send up stalks producing small, daisy-like flowers in clusters that may last for two to three months. Sometimes plants die after flowering but leave new growth in the form of offsets.

The black tree grows to 3 feet tall. The common name comes from the deep copper to purple color of the spatulate leaves, which are 2 to 3 inches long, ½ to ¾ inch wide and rounded at the tip. In late winter, golden-yellow flowers, ¾ inch across, appear in 4-inch-long clusters.

The pin wheel branches freely from the base, forming a dense, rounded shrub 1 to 2 feet tall and equally wide. Blue-green to gray-green leaves, covered with a waxy powder in summer, are edged with short red bristles. Oval in shape with pointed tips, the leaves are 1 to 2 inches long and ¾ to 1 inch wide. White to pale yellow flowers tinged with pink appear in early spring in clusters 4 to 5 inches long.

Aeoniums grow quickly. Their natural habitat is in the Southern Hemisphere, but they will also adapt to a spring-through-fall growth period indoors in the Northern Hemisphere. Aeoniums are undemanding house plants that can be grown on window sills in individual pots or in large dish gardens. Outdoors, aeoniums are grown in containers, in rock gardens and as a ground cover.

HOW TO GROW. For best growth indoors, aeoniums should get four or more hours of direct sunlight daily, or 12 or more hours of strong artificial light. They grow fairly well in bright indirect light, though with less vivid leaf colors. During active growth, night temperatures of 55° to 70° and day temperatures of 70° to 90° are recommended. Provide low or moderate humidity. Let the soil dry to the touch between thorough waterings when the plant is actively growing; when it is dormant, water just enough to keep it from shriveling.

Plant in a mixture of equal parts of commercial potting soil and sharp sand. To each gallon of mix, add 1 tablespoon of ground limestone and 1 tablespoon of bone meal. When new growth starts, feed once, using 1 teaspoon of bone meal to a 4- to 6-inch pot. Do not feed newly potted plants. Repot crowded plants just before new growth begins. Water lightly after repotting until new roots and leaves develop. Propagate from seeds or from stem cuttings taken at the beginning of

BLACK TREE
Aeonium arboreum atropurpureum

PIN WHEEL
Aeonium haworthii

For climate zones, see map, page 150.

93

VARIEGATED CENTURY PLANT
Agave americana marginata

Agave univittata

the growing season. Plants grow more vigorously and bloom more freely if they are taken out of their pots and planted in the garden during the summer months. Before frost in the fall, dig up the plants, trim back their roots and put them into pots the size they came from. Outdoors, aeoniums are hardy in Zone 10 and in very sheltered areas of Zone 9. They grow best in full sun and low humidity. The soil should be well drained; work ground limestone and bone meal into it before planting. When new growth begins, feed with a sprinkling of bone meal.

AGAVE

A. americana marginata (variegated century plant); *A. filifera* (thread-bearing century plant); *A. filifera compacta* (dwarf thread-bearing century plant); *A. parviflora; A. univittata; A. victoriae-reginae* (Queen Victoria century plant)
Size: Flower spikes 4 to 30 feet; leaves 4 inches to 5 feet

Native to North, Central and South America and the West Indies, century plants grow wild in areas as varied as ocean shorelines and high mountain regions. In size these succulents range from small to immense, but their slow growth allows even large species to serve as house plants when young. Century plants reach their maturity and bloom only after 10 to 50 years of growth, by which time they are usually several feet in diameter. Stemless or nearly so, the plants grow in rosettes of long, narrow leaves that have sharp teeth or threadlike growths along the edges and a pointed spine at each tip. The leaf colors are green, blue-green or gray-green, sometimes with white or cream markings. In the summer blooming period, blossoms line a single long many-branched flower stalk. Each bloom is bell-shaped, usually in shades of yellow-green. After it flowers and the seeds ripen, the plant dies, but offsets appear around its base.

A ground-hugging rosette, the variegated century plant has gray-green leaves edged in yellow with tips that bend downward. Each leaf can grow up to 5 feet long and 10 inches wide. At 10 to 25 years of age, the plant will send up a 6- to 25-foot stalk with 3½-inch clusters of fragrant flowers along its upper portion. The glossy green leaves of the thread-bearing century plant have thin, white, curly fibers lining the edges and a ½-inch needle-like tip. Growing up to 10 inches long and 1 inch wide, the stiff, upward-curving leaves form ground-hugging rosettes. Along most of the length of the 8-foot flower stem grow 2-inch yellow-green flowers that may turn maroon. The dwarf thread-bearing century plant has 4-inch leaves.

Another dwarf, *A. parviflora* has stiff, dark green leaves only 4 inches long and ½ inch wide; they split into threads near their tips. White lines mark the upper surface and the edges have teeth near the base. The flower spike can be 5 feet long with ⅝-inch yellow or green-yellow flowers. A native to northern Mexico and southern Arizona, *A. parviflora* is small, pretty and easy to grow as a house plant.

Straight and stiff, the 1- to 1½-foot-long, 1½-inch-wide leaves of *A. univittata* are green with a pale center stripe. Along the edges are ⅜-inch teeth, triangular with curved tips; at each leaf tip is a brown spine 1 inch long. The 10-foot flower spike has pale green flowers 2 inches long.

The Queen Victoria century plant, among the most decorative of the small plants, forms tightly packed, very symmetrical rosettes. The thick, stiff dark green leaves are 4 to 12 inches long and 1 to 3 inches wide with rounded tips. They have no teeth, but the edges as well as the undersides have rough white markings. Each leaf ends in a dark, blunt main spine and two smaller spines. Flower spikes may be 4 to 12 feet long with 2-inch pale green or yellow-green flowers.

The best species of agave for indoor use are the marginata, dwarf thread-bearing and Queen Victoria century plants and *A. parviflora*. Easy to grow when young, they are used in dish gardens or are grown in individual pots. Plants benefit from spending summers outdoors. Century plants make striking landscape plants in well-drained beds and borders.

HOW TO GROW. Indoors, century plants grow best where they get four or more hours of direct sunlight daily or 12 to 16 hours of strong artificial light. From spring through autumn, they need night temperatures of 65° to 70° and day temperatures of 75° to 95°. In winter, night temperatures of 45° to 50° and day temperatures under 65° are ideal. Keep humidity low. For best results, plant in a mixture of equal parts of commercial potting soil and sharp sand, adding 1 tablespoon of ground limestone and 1 tablespoon of bone meal to each gallon of mix. From spring through fall, let the soil become dry to the touch, then water thoroughly; in winter, water the plants only enough to keep their leaves from shriveling.

Feed established plants once each spring, using 1 teaspoon of bone meal to a 4- to 6-inch pot; do not feed newly potted plants the first year. Century plants seldom need repotting, but if they become overcrowded, repot in spring; wear gloves and use rolled newspapers to handle the prickly plants. Propagate from seeds or division of offsets, except for the Queen Victoria century plant, which can be started only from seeds.

Outdoors, century plants thrive in low humidity areas of Zones 7-10. Select a site with full sun. Grow in a well-drained sandy loam, working in ground limestone and bone meal before planting. Feed once each spring with bone meal.

AGAVE, WAX See *Echeveria*
AGAVE CACTUS See *Leuchtenbergia*

AICHRYSON

A. dichotomum, also called *A. laxum* and *Sempervivum annuum*; *A. domesticum* (youth-and-old-age)
Size: 6 inches to 1 foot tall

Relatives of *Sedum* and *Sempervivum*, these succulent plants are native to the Canary Islands. They are small, upright plants, which branch freely and have fleshy, spoon-shaped leaves. *A. dichotomum*, the most widely grown of the aichrysons, is an annual or biennial. The 1-foot-tall plants have erect, branching stems bearing almost circular leaves 1 to 3 inches long. In the late spring, pale yellow, ⅜-inch flowers appear. Youth-and-old-age is a perennial plant that grows up to 1 foot tall. Leaf clusters at the branch tips are dense and green; the leaves are ¾ inch long. Clusters of seven or eight yellow flowers slightly more than ½ inch wide open in the early summer.

The period of active growth for the perennials is from fall through spring; the plants are dormant in the summer. Indoors, they may change to a winter-dormancy pattern. Slow growing, they bloom one or two years after starting from seed or in one year from cuttings. Most species can be used indoors as house plants or outdoors in rock gardens.

HOW TO GROW. Aichrysons grow best indoors where they receive four or more hours of direct sunlight daily or 14 to 16 hours of artificial light, during the growing season, but they grow fairly well in bright indirect light such as that reflected from light walls. In the growing season, provide night temperatures of 65° to 70° and day temperatures of 75° to 85°; during dormancy, they need night temperatures of 50° to 55° and day temperatures of 65° or less. Humidity should be low to moderate. Let the soil become dry to the touch, then water thoroughly when the plants are in active growth; when

Aichryson dichotomum

For climate zones, see map, page 150.

they are resting, water only enough to keep the plants from shriveling. Feed established plants biweekly with a high-phosphorus fertilizer such as 15-30-15, diluted to one fourth the recommended strength. Do not feed newly potted plants the first year. For best results, plant in a mixture of equal parts of commercial potting soil and sharp sand; to each gallon of the mix, add 1 tablespoon of ground limestone and 1 tablespoon of bone meal. For faster growth, repot annually; otherwise, repot only when the plants become overcrowded, usually every three to five years. Plants may be propagated from seeds, leaf cuttings or offshoot rosettes.

Hardy outdoors in Zone 10, aichryson needs full sun, low to moderate humidity and well-drained sandy loam. Work bone meal and ground limestone into the soil before planting and feed each spring with bone meal.

ALLUAUDIA
A. humbertii
Size: Up to 10 feet tall

Native to arid regions of Madagascar, these freely branching, woody-stemmed succulents form treelike plants when they are mature. Sharp, needle-shaped spines ½ to 1 inch long are spaced ¼ to ½ inch apart along the gray-brown stems. Oval leaves, green or suffused with purple, appear along the stems. On new stems, leaves are horizontal; these drop in the fall, and the second year, on this old wood, leaves are vertical. Alluaudia grows slowly, attaining mature height of 6 to 10 feet only after 10 to 20 years. Indoors, alluaudia is a collector's plant, shown to best advantage in an individual pot. Outdoors, it blends well with other succulents and cacti in landscape or container plantings.

HOW TO GROW. *A. humbertii* grows best with four to six hours of direct sunlight daily or with 12 to 16 hours of strong artificial light, but it will grow fairly well in bright indirect light, such as that reflected from light walls. Bright light intensifies the purple coloration, but plants can become sunburned with light that is too intense. When the plants are actively growing, night temperatures of 65° to 70° and day temperatures of 75° to 85° are ideal. In the winter, night temperatures of 50° and day temperatures of 65° or lower are preferable. From spring through fall, let the soil become barely dry, then water thoroughly; in winter, water only enough to keep the plant from shriveling. Feed once each spring using 1 teaspoon of bone meal to a 4- to 6-inch pot. Do not feed newly potted plants the first year. Repot annually in early spring for fast growth; otherwise, repot in spring if plants become crowded. Use a mixture of 1 part commercial potting soil and 1 part sharp sand. To each gallon, add 1 tablespoon of ground limestone and 1 tablespoon of bone meal. Propagate from seeds or cuttings.

Alluaudia is hardy outdoors only in Zone 10. Plants grow best in full sun with low humidity. Grow in well-drained sandy loam. Work ground limestone and bone meal into the soil before planting. Feed once each spring with bone meal.

ALMONDS, SUGARED See *Pachyphytum*

ALOE
A. aristata (lace aloe); *A. brevifolia* (short-leaved aloe); *A. haworthiodes; A. humilis* (crocodile jaws, spider aloe); *A. nobilis* (gold-toothed aloe); *A. variegata* (tiger aloe); *A. vera,* also called *A. barbadensis* (true aloe)
Size: 2 inches to 6 feet tall

Aloes have been cultivated for centuries for both decorative and medicinal purposes. Succulent plants native mainly to the African continent and surrounding islands, aloes grow

Alluaudia humbertii

wild from ocean shores to mountainous areas and in both deserts and jungles. They form rosettes ranging from very small to treelike and often send up offsets. The thick, green, fleshy leaves are rounded on the bottom and curve inward on the surface; they are long, narrow, toothed along the edges and pointed at the tip. Emerging from between the leaves in winter, flower stalks have clusters of red, yellow or orange tubular flowers flaring at the ends into six petals.

The lace aloe is a stemless, 4- to 8-inch rosette with more than 100 leaves. Up to 4 inches long and ¾ inch wide, the gray- to blue-green leaves have horizontal bands of white bumps on the undersides and white teeth lining the edges and their tips bear long, thin bristles. Flower stalks up to 1½ feet tall have 20 or more red-to-yellow flowers, each 1¼ inches long. The short-leaved aloe, forming a rosette up to 6 inches across, has gray-green triangular leaves 3 inches long and 1 inch wide edged with white teeth. Plants send up 1½-foot-long flower stalks packed with 1½-inch-long red blooms.

A. haworthiodes, only 2 inches tall, has thin green leaves 1 to 2 inches long. Covered with white teeth, the leaves form small, dense rosettes. The 6-inch flower spike usually has more than a dozen tiny red flowers. Crocodile jaws has a stemless rosette formed from white-warted blue-green leaves 1 to 4 inches long and ¾ inch wide. The leaf edges have white teeth and curve upward toward spikes more than a foot tall with yellow flowers 1½ inches long. There are several varieties of this species, including one that turns purple in bright light.

Gold-toothed aloe has sprawling 2- to 6-foot stems with rosettes of leaves 8 to 12 inches long and 3 inches wide. Pale green to yellow-green, the leaves have pale, prickly teeth along the edges. Red flowers up to 1½ inches long appear in 18-inch clusters. Tiger aloe is one of the most attractive species. Its triangular leaves are deep, glossy green to blue-green with gray-green to white splotches in uneven cross-bands. Up to 6 inches long and 1½ inches wide, the leaves have rough white teeth along the edges. The rosettes of the tiger aloe grow to be 12 inches tall and 6 inches across. Foot-tall spikes have 1½-inch red flowers. The true aloe, long valued for the soothing quality of its sap, which is used in treating cuts and burns, has fleshy, bright green leaves up to 2 feet long. Soft white-to-red teeth edge the leaves, which have white spots when young. Stalks up to 3 feet tall bear 1-inch yellow or red flowers.

Most aloes are medium- to slow-growing plants. Some species flower when three years of age; others take five years or more to reach that stage.

The best house-plant choices are lace aloe, short-leaved aloe, *A. haworthiodes,* crocodile jaws and tiger aloe. Aloes are attractive in patio containers as well as in landscape planting or in a rock garden. Gold-toothed aloe is used in large groups in the landscape. Short-leaved aloe and crocodile jaws both make interesting ground covers.

HOW TO GROW. Most aloes grow best indoors where they get four or more hours a day of direct sunlight or 12 to 14 hours of strong artificial light. They will grow fairly well in bright indirect light. Lace aloe, *A. haworthiodes* and tiger aloe should get filtered sun in the summer. When actively growing, they need night temperatures of 50° to 55° and day temperatures of 68° to 72°; in winter, night temperatures of 45° to 50° and day temperatures of 60° to 65° are ideal. All species require low humidity. From spring through fall allow the soil to become dry to the touch, then water thoroughly. Less watering helps control the size of large species. In winter, water just enough to keep plants from shriveling. Miniatures that have reached flowering size should be wa-

CROCODILE JAWS
Aloe humilis

For climate zones, see map, page 150.

tered slightly more often. Feed established plants when new growth starts, using 1 teaspoon of bone meal to a 4- to 6-inch pot. Do not feed newly potted plants for the first year. Although aloes seldom need repotting, if plants are overcrowded repot when new growth is beginning. For best results use a mixture of commercial potting soil and sharp sand, adding to each gallon of mix 1 tablespoon of ground limestone and 1 tablespoon of bone meal. Plants growing in large tubs or containers should have the top soil replaced every two or three years. Although small, *A. haworthiodes* has a large root system that requires a pot to match. When repotting aloes, do not set them any deeper than they were previously growing. Propagate at any season from offsets or sow seeds in late winter or spring. Aloes with stems can be propagated from stem cuttings.

Aloes are hardy outdoors in Zone 10 and in protected areas of Zone 9. Grow in full sun except for crocodile jaws, which needs partial shade. Plants do best in low to moderate humidity. The soil must be well-drained sandy loam. Work ground limestone and bone meal into the soil before planting. Feed with bone meal each year when new growth begins.

ANACAMPSEROS

A. alstonii; A. buderana; A. tomentosa
Size: Up to 5 inches tall

These small, unusual succulents native to southern Africa have fleshy leaves and five-petaled flowers produced either individually or on branched stalks. Flowers open only in full sun and last only a short time. The stems of *A. alstonii* grow from the flat upper surface of a large, tuberous root. Only ½ inch tall, they appear in tufts, with each stem bearing minute leaves covered with silvery, pointed scales. The scales grow in five straight rows around each stem, which produces one white or cherry-colored flower ½ inch across. *A. buderana,* sometimes called silver worm, has twisting, creeping stems less than ¼ inch in diameter and branchlets ½ inch long. The stems are covered with silver scales and the small flowers are greenish-white. *A. tomentosa* produces several 2-inch-tall stems bearing ½-inch-long oval leaves with undersides covered with fine, soft, white hairs. A 2½-inch spike of three rosy flowers appears in midsummer.

HOW TO GROW. These species will grow indoors with four or more hours of filtered sunlight daily or up to eight hours of strong artificial light. From spring through fall, provide night temperatures of 55° to 70° and day temperatures of 70° to 90°. In winter, maintain night temperatures of 45° to 50° and day temperatures under 65°. Keep the humidity level low. Let the soil become barely dry between thorough waterings from spring through autumn; in winter, water just enough to keep plants from shriveling. Feed established plants once each spring, using 1 teaspoon of bone meal to a 4- to 6-inch pot. Do not feed newly potted plants. Pot in a mixture of equal parts commercial potting soil and sharp sand; to each gallon of the mixture, add 1 tablespoon of ground limestone and 1 tablespoon of bone meal. Propagate in spring from seeds or in spring and summer from cuttings.

APOROCACTUS

A. flagelliformis (rattail cactus)
Size: Up to 3 feet long and 1 inch thick when mature

A Mexican plant that hangs from trees or rocky mountain crevices, the rattail is one of the easiest of all cacti to grow. Its green cylindrical stems lengthen at the rate of 3 or 4 inches a year. They have eight to 15 narrow, rounded ribs, thickly covered with short, thin spines that are yellow or red-brown. The funnel-shaped pink-to-red flowers, 2 to 3 inches

Anacampseros alstonii

long, appear in spring, each one opening during the day and closing at night for three or four days. When the flowers fade, small red berries develop. Rattail cactus is attractively displayed on a pedestal or in a hanging basket. It can be successfully grafted onto upright-growing cacti. Hybrids have been developed that produce brighter red or pink flowers. Outdoors, the plant can be grown pendant or creeping over the ground and among rocks.

HOW TO GROW. For best growth, the rattail cactus should get four or more hours of direct sunlight a day or at least 12 hours of strong artificial light, but it grows fairly well in bright indirect light such as that reflected from light-colored walls. Light, during dormancy as well as growth periods, is the most important factor in producing flowers. From spring through autumn, night temperatures of 65° to 70° and day temperatures of 75° to 85° are ideal. In winter, night temperatures of 50° to 55° and day temperatures of 65° or less are best, although the plant tolerates lower temperatures. In late winter or in early spring, however, the plant should be moved to a warmer, sunnier location.

The plant grows best in a mixture of equal parts of commercial potting soil and sharp sand, with 1 tablespoon of ground limestone and 1 tablespoon of bone meal added to each gallon of the mix. From spring through autumn, the soil should become barely dry between thorough waterings; in winter, it needs only enough water to keep the plant from shriveling. An established plant should be fertilized once each spring with bone meal, but a newly potted plant should not be fed for the first year. Repotting annually in early spring will hasten growth, but the procedure is necessary only when the plant is overcrowded. Propagation is from seeds or stem cuttings in the summer. Outdoors, the rattail is hardy only in Zone 10. It grows best in a sunny location with low to moderate humidity. The soil should be a well-drained sandy loam, neutral to slightly alkaline.

APPLE CACTUS See *Cereus*

ARIOCARPUS
A. fissuratus (star cactus, living rocks)
Size: 2 to 6 inches in diameter when mature

This rare cactus is valued by collectors but is difficult to grow. Native to the deserts of southern Texas and northern and central Mexico, it produces fleshy leaflike tubercles in rosettes. Flowers appear near the center of the plant, closing at night and opening each morning. They last three or four days. The fleshy fruit, ½ to 1 inch long, is off-white to pale pink when ripe. The star cactus grows to a width of 6 inches with flowers almost 2 inches across.

HOW TO GROW. Star cactus is best grown indoors in individual pots. Outdoors, it should be displayed in a small rock garden. Grown indoors, it needs four or more hours a day of direct sunlight or strong artificial light 12 hours a day or more. Keep humidity levels low and temperatures at 50° to 55° nights and 65° to 75° days. If plants are dry, they can withstand winter temperatures as low as 45°. The soil must be very porous: 2 parts of sharp sand to 1 part leaf mold or commercial potting soil. Water even less than other cacti: in summer only on a bright, hot day when the soil is completely dry; in winter only if plants begin to shrivel. Feed in the spring with a teaspoon of bone meal to a 4- to 6-inch pot.

Although small in size, star cacti have large, tuberous roots that need plenty of room. If you select a large enough container the plant rarely needs repotting. In nature only the top surface shows, but in a pot it should be planted slightly above soil level to forestall rot. Propagate from cuttings.

For climate zones, see map, page 150.

RATTAIL CACTUS
Aporocactus flagelliformis

STAR CACTUS
Ariocarpus fissuratus

SAND DOLLAR
Astrophytum asterias

BISHOP'S CAP
Astrophytum myriostigma

Outdoors, star cacti are hardy in Zones 9 and 10. They require full sun and low humidity. Grow in a sandy loam. If the soil is acid, work ground limestone into it at planting time and fertilize lightly with bone meal in the spring.

ARTICHOKE CACTUS See *Obregonia*

ASTROPHYTUM
A. asterias (sand dollar, sea urchin); *A. capricorne* (goat-horn cactus); *A. myriostigma* (bishop's cap, monk's hood); *A. ornatum* (star cactus)
Size: 1½ to 14 inches tall

These small, fat cacti are found in the Mexican deserts and along the Rio Grande in Texas. Round to slightly columnar, the stem's five to eight ribs may be sharp-edged or rounded and are usually covered with coarse white flecks and edged with widely spaced, woolly areoles. Yellow, daisy-like flowers 1½ to 3½ inches across, some with red centers, emerge from the top of the plant in summer. Flowers usually last a week or more and are followed by scaly, globe-shaped fruit. Many hybrids and varieties are available.

The sand dollar, globe shaped and white flecked, is only 1½ inches tall and 3 inches across. It has eight shallow, rounded ribs. Although the plant is spineless, woolly areoles dominate it; they are evenly spaced along the ridges of the ribs. The 1½-inch flowers are yellow with red throats.

The goat-horn cactus slowly develops into a tapered column that is 4 inches thick and 10 inches tall. It usually has eight sharply defined ribs; in some varieties their green color is partially obscured by raised white flecks. The species gets its common name from flat, papery, 3-inch-long spines that twist and curve, as many as 10 of them from each areole. The plants must be handled carefully, since the fragile spines are easily broken off. The silky, 3-inch yellow flower has a throat suffused with red.

The bishop's cap is usually seen as a 2- to 8-inch globe, although it grows 2 feet tall and 8 inches across in its natural habitat. The five broad ribs are spineless but covered with fine, small gray specks. Woolly brown areoles line the ridges. The yellow flowers are 2½ inches long. The star cactus, with eight spirally arranged ribs, eventually becomes 6 inches in diameter and more than 12 inches in height. Flocked with thick, silver specks, the plants have clumps of 10 curved, yellow, stiff, sharp spines about 1¼ inches long. Their spectacular, bright yellow flowers are up to 3½ inches across.

These species grow slowly; from seed they will take four or five years to reach 2 to 3 inches in diameter. At this size they usually begin to bloom. They are popular indoor plants because their appearance is unusual and they are relatively easy to care for and bring into flower. They can be grown in individual pots or in dish gardens. Where climate permits they can grow outdoors year round.

HOW TO GROW. Indoors, astrophytums grow best where they get four or more hours a day of sunlight or at least 12 hours of strong artificial light, but they grow fairly well in bright indirect light. Intense summer sun can damage the plants. From spring through fall, night temperatures of 65° to 70° and day temperatures of 75° to 85° are recommended. In winter, night temperatures of 45° to 50° and day temperatures of 65° or less are ideal. Low humidity is essential.

In spring and fall the soil should become almost totally dry before the plant is thoroughly watered; in hot sunny summer weather, the soil should dry only moderately before the plant is watered. In winter, plants should be watered only enough to keep them from shriveling; the cooler the temperatures, the less water needed. Special care should be taken with plants under three years of age or 2 inches in diameter because they are susceptible to injury from overwatering.

Established plants should be fed once each spring with 1 teaspoon of bone meal to a 4- to 6-inch pot; newly potted plants should not be fertilized the first year. The potting soil should be a mixture of 1 part commercial potting soil and 1 part sharp sand. To each gallon of the mixture, add 1 tablespoon of ground limestone and 1 tablespoon of bone meal. Overcrowded plants should be repotted in spring. Propagate from seeds, handling them carefully.

Sand dollar, bishop's cap and star cactus are hardy in Zone 10; goat-horn cactus is also hardy in Zone 9. All should grow in full sun and low humidity. The soil should be a well-drained sandy loam, with ground limestone and bone meal worked into the soil before planting. Plants should be fertilized once each spring with bone meal.

B

BABY TOES See *Mesembryanthemum*
BACKBONE, DEVIL'S See *Pedilanthus*
BALL CACTUS See *Notocactus*
BALLS, GOLF See *Epithelantha*
BARBADOS GOOSEBERRY See *Pereskia*
BARREL CACTUS See *Echinocactus* and *Ferocactus*
BASKETBALL EUPHORBIA See *Euphorbia*
BEAR'S TOES See *Cotyledon*

BEAUCARNEA

B. recurvata, also called *Nolina recurvata* and *N. tuberculata* (pony tail, elephant-foot tree)
Size: To 30 feet tall

A succulent native to dry regions of Texas and Mexico, the pony tail is a favorite house plant because it thrives with very little attention. The lower stem is a swollen reservoir of water. As the plant ages, the upper stem elongates, forming a narrow trunk topped with leaves ¾ inch wide and up to 4 feet long. This cluster of drooping, twisting leaves gives the pony tail its common name. Spikes of small white flowers are produced infrequently. Indoor growth is slow, less than an inch each year. Outdoors or in a greenhouse, the plant grows slightly faster and eventually can attain a height of 30 feet. The spring and summer are the seasons of active growth. Pony tails are grown indoors as foliage plants; outdoors, they are planted in tubs for display on terraces and in the garden as small trees.

HOW TO GROW. The pony tail grows with four or more hours of sunlight daily or with strong artificial light for 12 hours or more a day; it grows fairly well in bright indirect light reflected from light-colored walls. Night temperatures of 50° to 55° and day temperatures of 68° to 72° are ideal, with slightly lower temperatures in winter. Plants survive temperatures from 40° to 90°. High humidity is unnecessary, but the leaves should be misted frequently to keep the tips from turning brown.

Grow the plant in packaged potting soil. Feed an established plant once a month in spring and summer with an indoor foliage-plant fertilizer such as 10-20-10, used according to package directions; wait a year before feeding a newly purchased or newly potted plant. Beaucarnea seldom needs repotting and can grow for years in a small container. When a plant becomes overcrowded, repot in early spring before new growth starts. Use a slightly larger pot and remove old soil from the base of the plant but avoid exposing the roots. Propagate from seeds in the spring.

A pony tail can grow outdoors year round in Zone 10. They grow best in full sun with a dry atmosphere. The soil

PONY TAIL
Beaucarnea recurvata

For climate zones, see map, page 150.

should be a sandy loam with limestone and a balanced fertilizer added at planting. Feed once each spring with 10-10-10 fertilizer mixed into the soil surface.

BIRD'S-NEST CACTUS See *Mammillaria*
BIRD'S-NEST SANSEVIERIA See *Sansevieria*
BISHOP'S CAP See *Astrophytum*
BLACK TREE See *Aeonium*
BLUE FLAME See *Myrtillocactus*
BOOJUM TREE See *Fouquiera*

BOWIEA
B. volubilis (climbing onion)
Size: Trailing stems 6 feet long

This southern African succulent, a member of the lily family, is an unusual vinelike plant. The 3- to 7-inch green, onion-like bulb grows near the top of the soil, and out of the bulb grow slender, twining green stems 3 to 6 feet long, which branch and rebranch. Six-pointed star-shaped flowers, ⅝ inch across and green-white, appear at the tips of the branches in late winter. Each year, in the active growing season from autumn through winter, the stems attain their full height, then die back, leaving the bulb dormant in the spring and summer. The climbing onion is grown indoors trailing from a suspended container; outdoors, it is best displayed on a trellis.

HOW TO GROW. Climbing onion needs at least four hours of direct sun daily or very bright artificial light for 12 hours; it will grow fairly well in bright indirect light. Give it night temperatures of 50° to 55° and day temperatures of 68° to 72° in winter; during summer dormancy, night temperatures of 40° to 45° and day temperatures of 50° to 55° are best if they can be achieved; otherwise keep climbing onion between 65° and 90° the year round. Use equal parts of commercial potting soil and sharp sand, with 1 tablespoon of ground limestone and 1 tablespoon of bone meal added to each gallon of the mixture. Allow the soil to become moderately dry between thorough waterings when the plant is actively growing. As the branches begin to turn yellow, reduce watering and discontinue watering altogether while the bulb is dormant.

Feed the plant in autumn as new growth begins, adding 1 teaspoon of bone meal to a 4- to 6-inch pot. Plants seldom need repotting but when it is necessary, repot in the fall, putting only one quarter of the bulb into the soil. Propagate from seeds. Climbing onion will grow outdoors in Zone 10. It needs full sun and low humidity. Plant it in a well-drained sandy loam. Work ground limestone and bone meal into the soil before planting, and feed the plant in the fall with bone meal. In spring and summer, cover the bulb to keep it dry.

BRACT, SILVER See *Pachyphytum*
BRAIN CACTUS See *Echinofossulocactus*
BUGLER, SCARLET See *Cleistocactus*
BUNNY EARS See *Opuntia*
BURRO'S TAIL See *Sedum*

BURSERA
B. microphylla (elephant tree)
Size: 4 to 10 feet tall

Native to the desert hills of Arizona, California and northwest Mexico, the elephant tree is an oddly shaped succulent: its base is a swollen trunk covered with pale bark that buckles and splits off. Rising and spreading from the trunk are reddish, straggly branches and twigs. The deciduous, 1½-inch-long compound leaves are composed of up to 33

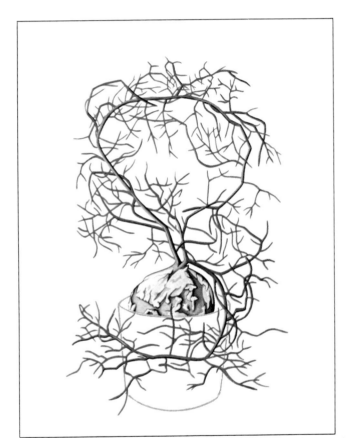

CLIMBING ONION
Bowiea volubilis

strongly scented leaflets, each ¼ inch long. Clusters of small yellow flowers appear before the leaves in spring. Elephant tree grows very slowly. Indoors, the plant is usually grown for the same kind of display as bonsai. Outdoors, it is grown in pots or as a landscape specimen.

HOW TO GROW. The elephant tree grows best indoors in a location where it gets four or more hours of direct sunlight daily or 12 to 16 hours of strong artificial light, but it will grow fairly well in bright indirect light. During the hottest months of summer the sunlight should be lightly filtered. From spring through fall, night temperatures of 65° to 70° and day temperatures of 75° to 85° with low humidity are recommended. In winter, night temperatures of 50° and day temperatures of 65° or less are best.

A mixture of equal parts of commercial potting soil and sharp sand should be used with 1 tablespoon of ground limestone and 1 tablespoon bone meal added to each gallon of potting mix. From spring through fall, let the soil become barely dry to the touch between thorough waterings. In winter, the soil should dry thoroughly before the plant is watered. In spring feed established plants with 1 teaspoon of bone meal to a 4- to 6-inch pot. Newly potted plants should not be fed the first year. Repotting is seldom necessary, but when a plant is overcrowded, repot in early spring. Elephant tree can be propagated from seed or from stem cuttings in spring or summer.

This succulent is hardy outdoors only in Zone 10 and grows best in full sun or filtered shade with low humidity. The soil should be a well-drained sandy loam, with ground limestone and bone meal worked into it before planting. Fertilize each spring with bone meal.

BUSH, RAINBOW See *Portulacaria*
BUTTON CACTUS See *Epithelantha*
BUTTONS, STRING-OF- See *Crassula*

C

CANDELILLA See *Euphorbia*
CAP, DWARF TURK'S See *Melocactus*

CARALLUMA
C. europaea; C. rogersii
Size: 4 inches tall

These small succulents are native to arid regions bordering the Mediterranean. In their natural habitat clumps grow in sandy or rocky soil, usually in the shade of larger desert shrubs. Branching from the base, the generally leafless gray or green stems are short, four-sided with blunt teeth and of an even ¾-inch thickness. The fleshy flowers range in size from ⅛ inch to 5 inches across; they appear singly or in clusters. *C. europaea* flowers, shaped like a fat, five-pointed star, are dark purple, banded with pale yellow around their centers. About ¾ inch wide, they grow in clusters of five to eight at or near the stem tips. They have a slightly unpleasant odor. *C. rogersii* produces pale yellow flowers 1½ inches wide that grow three or four to a cluster. These succulents grow actively from spring through late summer and are dormant in winter. Blooming occurs in the summer outdoors or in a greenhouse; the plants rarely bloom indoors. Plants started from seed usually flower in two or three years. If started from cuttings they may blossom in the first year. Both species are easy-to-grow house plants, excellent in dish gardens with cacti and other succulents.

HOW TO GROW. These small succulents grow well in bright indirect or curtain-filtered sunlight. When actively growing, the plants require night temperatures of 65° to 70° and day

ELEPHANT TREE
Bursera microphylla

Caralluma europaea

For climate zones, see map, page 150.

SAGUARO
Carnegiea gigantea

GOLDEN OLD-MAN CACTUS
Cephalocereus chrysacanthus

temperatures of 75° to 85°. In winter, night temperatures should be 40° to 45° and day temperatures 55° to 60°. The plants grow well in a mixture of equal parts of commercial potting soil and sharp sand, with 1 tablespoon of bone meal and 1 tablespoon of ground limestone added per gallon of the mixture. The soil should feel dry to the touch before thorough watering but should be kept slightly moist in very hot weather. In winter, water only if the plants start to shrivel. An established plant in a 6-inch pot needs feeding once each spring with 1 teaspoon of bone meal; a newly potted plant should not be fertilized for the first year. Repot crowded plants in late winter. *Caralluma* species can be started from fresh seed; the seeds germinate in less than a week if given a warm, moist environment. Or plants can be propagated from cuttings in early summer. The cuttings should be allowed to dry for two weeks before they are inserted in a potting mix.

Outdoors, the plant is hardy in Zone 10 in places where the humidity is low. It should be planted in filtered sun or partial shade. The soil, ideally slightly alkaline sandy loam, may need to have ground limestone and bone meal worked into it. Feed each spring with bone meal.

CARNEGIEA
C. gigantea (saguaro, giant saguaro)
Size: Up to 60 feet tall and 2 feet thick

Among the largest and slowest growing of all cacti, this native of the southwestern United States and northwestern Mexico was named after industrialist Andrew Carnegie. The immense cactus has an erect, columnar trunk that branches upward like a candelabra, with 12 to 30 ribs on each stem or branch. The saguaro has two kinds of spines: those on the lower part of the plant are straight or curved, gray and ½ to 3 inches long; those on newer growth are straight and yellow. In spring and summer white trumpet-shaped flowers 4 to 5 inches long open in the evening and close the following afternoon. After the flowers fade, edible red fruits develop, oval in shape and 2 to 3 inches long. The saguaro grows about 6 inches tall in its first 10 years, first blooms at about age 40 and begins to branch at about age 75 when it is 15 feet tall. Plants attain full size only after about 150 years.

HOW TO GROW. Indoors, saguaro seedlings need four to six hours of direct sunlight daily or 12 to 16 hours of strong artificial light. Keep night temperatures at 60° to 75° and day temperatures at 75° to 95° in the growing season. In winter keep night temperatures at 40° to 55° and day temperatures at 60° to 80°. Let soil become dry to the touch between thorough waterings in spring and summer; water even less in winter. Pot in 1 part sharp sand and 1 part commercial potting soil. In spring and summer feed established plants every two months with a foliage-plant fertilizer such as 10-20-10 diluted to half the strength recommended on the label. Although hardy in Zones 9 and 10, the saguaro does not adapt well to outdoor cultivation. Its root system is too shallow to secure it against wind, and it is very susceptible to injury from sudden frosts. If the large amount of water stored inside the plant freezes, the cells rupture and die, leaving large areas of dead tissue. If growing tips freeze, the plant dies or becomes misshapen. Propagate from seed.

CARPOBROTUS See *Mesembryanthemum*
CARRION FLOWER See *Stapelia*
CENTURY PLANT See *Agave*

CEPHALOCEREUS
C. chrysacanthus (golden old-man cactus); *C. senilis* (old-man cactus)

Size: 8 to 16 inches indoors; up to 50 feet in the wild

These popular cacti are native to a wide area in tropical and subtropical America, including the Florida Keys, the West Indies, Mexico, Ecuador and Brazil. The plants are found in climates ranging from warm, moist ocean shores to hot, dry mountains. In the wild they may grow to 40 feet in about 200 years; house plants are usually not over 12 inches tall. The upright, columnar stem has deep ribs and closely set spines, but the outstanding feature is a covering of gray or white hairs up to 5 inches long, so thick that it sometimes conceals the spines. Trumpet-shaped flowers with short, narrow petals of white, pink, red or purple last only one night. With the faded flower still attached to the plant, a globular fruit develops, which, when ripe, splits open to reveal colored pulp and small black seeds.

The golden old-man cactus grows 15 to 18 feet tall in the wild. The blue-green stems have 9 to 12 ribs and clumps of 12 to 15 golden spines up to 1½ inches long and spaced ⅜ inch apart under long white wool. The 3-inch long, rose-red flowers are followed by 1½-inch fruits with red skin and flesh. The old-man cactus, a favorite house plant since World War I, grows 50 feet tall and 1 foot in diameter in its native habitat. Up to 30 shallow, closely set ribs are covered with 2- to 12-inch white or gray hairs and thin, yellow spines 1½ inches long. The top of the plant has an especially thick covering of woolly fleece. From this area 2-inch pink flowers emerge. The oblong fruit is rose-colored and 1¼ inches long. Since these cacti grow slowly, young specimens are appropriate both for dish gardens and for single display in pots. But the plants do not bloom until they are 15 to 25 feet tall.

HOW TO GROW. These cacti grow best indoors where they get four or more hours of direct sunlight daily or 12 to 14 hours of strong artificial light, but they will grow fairly well in bright indirect light. Older plants with large amounts of hair can withstand bright sunlight better than young plants. In spring, summer and fall, night temperatures of 65° to 70° and day temperatures of 75° to 85° are ideal. In the winter, night temperatures of 45° to 50° and day temperatures of 65° or lower are needed. The old-man cactus can withstand winter temperatures that are slightly lower. The plants need moderate to high humidity when actively growing, but low humidity in winter. Let the soil become dry to the touch before watering thoroughly from spring through autumn; in winter, water only enough to keep plants from shriveling.

Fertilize established plants once each spring, using 1 teaspoon of bone meal to a 4- to 6-inch pot. Do not feed newly potted plants the first year. Pot in a mixture of equal parts of commercial potting soil and sharp sand, adding 1 tablespoon each of ground limestone and bone meal to each gallon of potting mix. For quickest growth, repot young plants annually in early spring. Otherwise, repot in spring only when plants become crowded, using a slightly larger container. Some growers cut and root young growth of the old-man cactus when its hairs lose their silver color. Propagate from fresh seed or cuttings taken in spring or summer.

Outdoors, these cacti are hardy only in Zones 9 and 10. Plant where they will receive full sun and moderate humidity in the growing season. Grow in well-drained sandy loam. Work ground limestone and bone meal into the soil before planting and feed once each spring with bone meal.

PERUVIAN APPLE CACTUS
Cereus peruvianus

CEREUS
C. peruvianus (Peruvian apple cactus); *C. peruvianus monstrosus* (giant club)
Size: Up to 40 feet tall in the wild; 10 inches to 3 feet tall as a house plant

For climate zones, see map, page 150.

Tough and vigorous, these cylindrical cacti are native to much of eastern South America as well as the West Indies, occurring from sea level to high in the mountains. Most species grow upright and branch freely, forming shrubby or treelike plants. Thin, deep ribs are waxy green or blue-green and have widely spaced circular areoles covered with white or brown wool; the gray, black or brown spines are needle-shaped. Blooming at night, large funnel-shaped white, pink or green-white flowers develop along the old growth of the stems. Round or oval, the edible fruits are a bright, shiny red with purple, white or red flesh inside.

The Peruvian apple cactus, found in nature from 10 to 40 feet tall, usually branches in cultivation when the growing tips are pruned back. Stems up to 4 inches thick are blue- to gray-green with six to eight sharp ribs that are 2 inches deep. These are edged with groups of brown to black spines ¾ to 2 inches long, spaced 1 inch apart. The 6½-inch flowers have a slight fragrance. A slightly flattened globe, the 2½-inch fruit is yellow tinged with red on the outside and white inside. The giant club cactus, a mutation, grows slowly, forming new heads on its irregularly bulging columns. These are green- to blue-green with black or brown spines. In summer, large white nocturnal flowers appear.

With room for roots to spread and a propitious environment, cereus will grow quickly outdoors, adding 1 to 2 feet each year. Indoors, plants will grow several inches each year, becoming up to 3 feet tall. Large cereus plants are useful for interior decorating. Outdoors, one may serve as a display plant at the back of a cactus and succulent garden, or a number may be planted to form a hedge. Cereus species are also widely used as the erect stock for grafting.

HOW TO GROW. Cereus species grow best indoors where they get four or more hours a day of direct sunlight or at least 12 hours of strong artificial light. Seedlings, however, grow better if lighted indirectly because very bright light can sometimes burn them. When actively growing in the spring, summer and autumn, give cereus night temperatures of 60° to 70° and day temperatures of 70° to 90°. In winter, night temperatures of 40° to 50° and day temperatures below 70° are ideal. Species from the West Indies should have winter temperatures at the upper end of the range.

Plants grow best in a dry atmosphere in soil that is a mixture of 1 part commercial potting soil and 1 part sharp sand. To each gallon of the mixture, add 1 tablespoon of ground limestone and 1 tablespoon of bone meal. Let the soil become dry to the touch between thorough waterings from spring through fall; in winter, water only enough to keep plants from shriveling. Fertilize established plants once each spring, using 1 teaspoon of bone meal to a 4- to 6-inch pot. Do not feed newly potted plants the first year. Repot annually in early spring for quickest growth; otherwise, repot in spring when plants become crowded. Bedded outdoors in summer, some species will flower. To miniaturize plants, keep them in the same size pot, trimming back the roots each spring. Propagate from fresh seeds or stem cuttings.

Outdoors, these plants are hardy in Zone 10. They grow rapidly and may quickly outgrow the space set aside for them. Plants grow best with full sun and low humidity. Soil should be a well-drained sandy loam. Work ground limestone and bone meal into the soil before planting. Feed cereus plants once each spring with bone meal.

CEROPEGIA
C. woodii (rosary vine, heart vine)
Size: Trailing stems 3 feet long

The slender stems of this trailing southern African succu-

ROSARY VINE
Ceropegia woodii

lent grow from bulblike tubers. On the stems are pairs of heart-shaped leaves mottled with silver that prompt most of the plant's common names. In fall, 1-inch purple flowers form in small clusters at the leaf joints; the plant may bloom as long as six weeks. In late winter, seed pods form. When they burst, the air is filled with tiny soft balls that resemble milkweed. The rosary vine is a rapid grower, extending 2 to 4 feet in a single year, mostly during the spring and summer. Growth slows in winter.

HOW TO GROW. Although it will tolerate reduced light, the rosary vine does best in indirect or curtain-filtered sunlight. Temperatures of 50° to 55° at night and 68° to 72° by day are ideal. Let the soil become moderately dry between thorough waterings from spring through fall; in winter, water only enough to keep leaves from shriveling. Feed twice a month from spring until midsummer with a low-nitrogen fertilizer, such as 5-10-10, diluted to half the strength that is recommended on the label. Repot overcrowded plants in the spring, using a mixture of equal parts of commercial potting soil and sharp sand; add 1 tablespoon of ground limestone and 1 tablespoon of bone meal to each gallon of potting mix. Do not fertilize newly potted plants the first year. Propagate in spring by potting stem cuttings or the tiny tubers that form at the leaf joints.

CHAIN CACTUS See *Rhipsalis*

CHAMAECEREUS
C. silvestrii (peanut cactus)
Size: Stems to 6 inches long

Peanut cactus is native to western Argentina. Creeping, low-lying stems branch from the base and are generally about ½ inch thick. The cylindrical stems have six to nine ribs, which are studded with short white bristles. When the plant is placed in a bright summer light, the pale green stems may turn violet. Funnel-shaped flowers up to 3 inches long appear in spring.

HOW TO GROW. This cactus should have bright light year round; otherwise it will become distorted, leggy and pale. To ensure spring flowering, keep late autumn and winter temperatures between 45° and 55°. In spring and summer, 65° to 95° temperatures are required. Peanut cactus does well in a mixture of equal parts of commercial potting soil and sharp sand. Allow the top half of the soil to become dry between thorough waterings in spring and summer. In fall and winter, when the plant is dormant, water only enough so it does not shrivel. Fertilize with high-phosphorus fertilizer such as 15-30-15 once a month during spring and summer. Dilute the fertilizer as recommended on the label. Repot with care in the spring; the stems are very fragile.

Propagate by detaching and rooting small stem cuttings. Peanut cactus does not set seed; all the plants that are sold in the United States and Canada are descended from a single clone that was imported years ago.

CHICKENS, HEN-AND- See *Sempervivum*
CHIN CACTUS See *Gymnocalycium*
CHINESE RUBBER PLANT See *Crassula*
CHOLLA See *Opuntia*
CHRISTMAS CACTUS See *Schlumbergera*

CISSUS
C. quadrangularis (Veldt ivy); *C. trifoliata* (possum grape)
Size: Stems to 8 feet long

These quick-growing climbing succulents are commonly cultivated in hanging pots or trained on trellises. They have

PEANUT CACTUS
Chamaecereus silvestrii

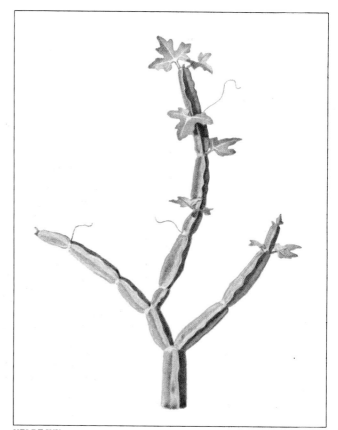

VELDT IVY
Cissus quadrangularis

For climate zones, see map, page 150.

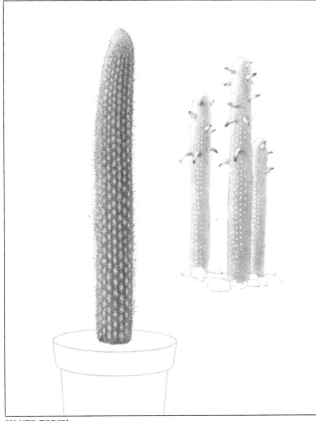

SILVER TORCH
Cleistocactus strausii

Conophytum minutum

tendrils and sparse grapelike leaves. The segmented stems are thick, fleshy and smooth with projecting wings. Veldt ivy is native to southern Africa. It has ribbed stems with sparse, grapelike leaves 2 inches long. Its infrequent flowers appear in late summer or early fall in loose, light-green clusters on stubby stalks. Pea-sized red berries may appear in the fall if the flowers are pollinated. Possum grape is a low-climbing vine from tropical South America with stout inch-long tendrils. Slightly toothed leaflets grow in groups of three. Both leaves and clumps of tiny green flowers are about 2½ inches long. The berries are dark purple or black.

HOW TO GROW. Veldt ivy and possum grape need bright light and temperatures that never fall below 50°. Both species tend to follow the inverted seasonal cycle of the Southern Hemisphere, becoming dormant in summer and growing actively in winter, though they may change under cultivation. Allow soil to dry almost completely when the plant is dormant. When it is active, keep the soil slightly moist and feed every two weeks with a balanced house-plant fertilizer, such as 20-20-20, diluted to one half the strength that is recommended on the label. Propagate from stem cuttings during the growing season.

CLEFT STONE See *Pleiospilos*

CLEISTOCACTUS
C. baumannii (scarlet bugler); *C. strausii* (silver torch)
Size: To 6 feet tall when mature

These South American cacti are slender, columnar plants. When they have reached 5 feet in height they produce orange or red flowers, S-shaped on the scarlet bugler, tubular on the silver torch. Blooms open only wide enough for the stamens to protrude, hence the Latin name meaning closed cactus. Scarlet bugler has 1½-inch-thick stems, branching near the base, with close-set areoles. It is thickly covered with yellow wool and yellow-to-dark brown spines about 1 inch long. Blossoms are 2 to 3 inches long. The plant usually requires support when it nears its maximum height of 6 feet. Silver torch has close-set woolly areoles and many short, white hairlike spines. Flowers are commonly 3½ inches long. The mature plant is 5 to 6 feet tall.

HOW TO GROW. Both species grow best in bright light with indoor temperatures from 50° to 55° in winter and 65° to 90° in summer. However, both species will thrive outside in Zones 9 and 10 and in Zone 8 from central Texas westward if they are kept almost completely dry over the winter. As house plants, these cacti winter well on an enclosed porch or in a cool greenhouse; in summer they should sit in an open window with good light or be put outdoors in direct sunlight or very light shade. Pot in an alkaline soil mix of equal parts commercial potting soil and sharp sand. Water when soil is nearly dried out in the spring and summer growing season; in winter, water only enough to keep the plants from shriveling. Feed monthly in spring and summer with a high-phosphorus fertilizer, such as 15-30-15, following the instructions given on the label. The plants are vigorous and easily raised from seed or from stem cuttings. Six-inch-high cuttings will double in size in a year, with most of the growth taking place in the summer; in fall and winter the plants are dormant. Both species make excellent grafting stock.

CLIMBING ONION See *Bowiea*
CLUB, GIANT See *Cereus*
COB CACTUS See *Lobivia*
COBWEB HOUSELEEK See *Sempervivum*
COMMON HOUSELEEK See *Sempervivum*

CONOPHYTUM

C. minutum, also called *Mesembryanthemum minutum; C. springbokense*

Size: ½ to 1 inch tall

Almost 300 species of this southern African dwarf succulent exist. They are nearly stemless—with fleshy green leaves growing in snug pairs. Flowers emerge from between these leaves. All of the species form new leaves within old ones. When the plant is dormant, the old leaves dry to a thin shell; when growth resumes, the shell splits and new leaves emerge. Clumps are formed when two pairs of leaves develop within an old pair. *C. minutum* is aptly named, for it is only ⅔ inch tall with gray-green to blue-green leaves that form a slightly convex top. The petals of its ½-inch flowers are magenta. *C. springbokense* has smooth, green, two-lobed leaves 1 inch high and ¾ inch wide. The ¾-inch flowers are a golden yellow.

In their native climate, with its inverted seasonal cycle, conophytum species grow and blossom during the winter. However, they may switch in Northern Hemisphere cultivation, with growth occurring in early spring and flowers appearing in summer.

HOW TO GROW. Indoors, conophytum needs bright but filtered light and temperatures between 60° and 90° year round. Flowers of most species open during the day, but some are nocturnal. The soil mixture—2 parts sharp sand to 1 part commercial potting soil—should be kept dry from January to June, with one March watering to prevent shriveling. In summer, mist lightly once a week; in fall, water once a week. Conophytum is easily propagated from seeds or by dividing clumps.

CORYPHANTHA

C. clava, also called *Mammillaria clava; C. missouriensis* (Missouri pincushion)

Size: 2½ to 12 inches tall and 3 to 4 inches thick

Species of these cacti can be found growing wild as far north as Alberta, Canada, and as far south as central Mexico. They are often confused with those of the *Mammillaria* genus but differ from them by flowering near the apex on new growth rather than below the apex on older growth. *C. clava* is a club-shaped desert cactus with yellow, brown or red spines; it grows 12 inches tall and 4 inches thick. Its yellow flowers are large (up to 3½ inches across) and bloom in summer. The Missouri pincushion received its name from the Missouri River that flows near the site where the cactus was discovered. Its stems grow 2½ inches high and 3 inches thick. The spines of young plants are covered with white hairs so fine that they are visible only with a hand lens. In spring, this grassland cactus produces fragrant yellow-green flowers ½ inch across.

HOW TO GROW. Indoors or out, these cacti need four hours or more of bright sunlight daily. From spring through early fall, allow soil to dry thoroughly before watering; in winter, water only if the plants begin to shrivel. They grow best with spring and summer day temperatures of 80° to 90° and night temperatures of 60° to 70°. In winter, the plants should be cool but the temperature should not drop below 40°. Plant in 2 parts sharp sand to 1 part commercial potting soil. Desert varieties have long taproots and need deep containers to permit the roots to develop properly. Watch carefully to avoid dampness that could cause rot. Feed every two months from spring through summer with a high-phosphorus fertilizer such as 15-30-15, following recommendations on the label; do not fertilize in winter. Propagate from seed. Outdoors, *C. clava* is hardy in Zones 8-10, the Missouri pincushion in

For climate zones, see map, page 150.

Conophytum springbokense

Coryphantha clava

SILVER CROWN
Cotyledon undulata

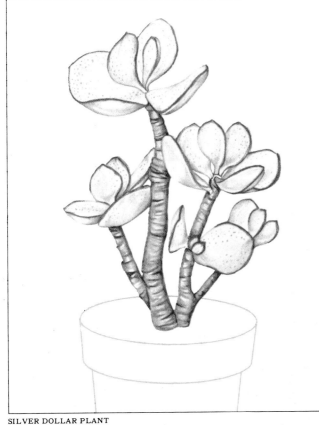

SILVER DOLLAR PLANT
Crassula arborescens

Zones 6-10. Plant in full sun in very sandy loam. Fertilize with a sprinkling of bone meal once a year in spring.

COTYLEDON

C. ladysmithiensis (bear's toes); *C. undulata* (silver crown)
Size: 1 to 2 feet tall

These succulents from southern Africa have a natural winter growing cycle, but in cultivation cotyledons may switch over to a normal summer schedule in the Northern Hemisphere. Bear's toes are bushy, growing to 1 foot high, and are covered with crowded, wedge-shaped leaves that are 2½ inches long and ¾ inch wide. Stems and leaves are silver-gray and are covered with a fine, soft fuzz. Clumps of creeping shoots have erect tips. The plant rarely flowers in cultivation. Silver crown has short-stemmed leaves, slender at the base, but widening to the size of a silver dollar with graceful undulating margins. These leaves are green but are covered with a mealy white dust. The inch-long drooping flowers are orange or red and blossom in the summer. In some parts of California, silver crown is sometimes used as a ground cover. As an indoor plant, it will grow to a height of 1 foot in a 6-inch pot.

HOW TO GROW. Bear's toes and silver crown need bright light and grow best with temperatures of 65° to 90° all year. When the plants are actively growing, usually in fall and winter, let the top half of the soil in the pot become dry to the touch between waterings; water even more sparingly when plants are dormant. Be careful not to drip water on silver-crown foliage; it will wash off the natural dustlike coating and spoil the plant's appearance. Cotyledons require a loose, well-drained soil, such as a mixture of equal parts of sharp sand and commercial potting soil. When the plants are growing, feed them biweekly with a high-phosphorus fertilizer, such as 15-30-15, diluted to one fourth the strength suggested on the label. Propagate from seeds or cuttings.

Outdoors, the plants can survive a drop in temperature to 40° if the soil is dry. They are hardy only in Zone 10.

COTYLEDON See also *Echeveria*
COW'S HORN See *Euphorbia*
CRAB CACTUS See *Schlumbergera* and *Zygocactus*

CRASSULA

C. arborescens, also called *C. cotyledon* (silver dollar plant); *C. argentea* (jade plant, Chinese rubber plant); *C. falcata* (scarlet paint brush, propeller plant); *C. lycopodioides* (rattail crassula); *C. perforata* (necklace vine, string-of-buttons)
Size: 2 inches to 3 feet tall

These easy-to-grow succulent house plants belong to a large family of almost 300 species, mostly natives of southern Africa. The silver dollar plant has rounded, gray leaves, often edged with red; its tiny flowers are white when they open, later turning red. The jade plant grows 10 feet tall in the wild, but even a 10-inch-high potted plant looks like a tiny tree. Varieties of the jade plant have 1- to 2-inch fleshy leaves that are shiny green or marked with combinations of white, yellow, orange, pink, red and purple. Outdoors in a mild climate like that of Southern California, the jade plant bears white or pink flowers, but it seldom blooms indoors.

Both the scarlet paint brush and the propeller plant are apt names for *C. falcata;* the 3- to 4-inch-wide flower heads are brush-shaped, and the long gray-green leaves, growing from top to bottom of the 2-foot stem, do look like propeller blades. Rattail crassula has creeping 6- to 24-inch-long stems thickly covered with small scalelike leaves; these are arranged in four rows, giving the stems a four-sided effect.

Minute white flowers appear between the leaves. Necklace vine grows to a height of 2 feet; pairs of 1-inch pointed leaves are strung necklace-like along upright stems. Crassulas flower outdoors from midwinter to early spring; but with the exception of scarlet paint brush, they rarely bloom as house plants and are valued for their shape and foliage.

HOW TO GROW. Crassulas grow best if given bright light year round, but filtered sunlight and indirect light, such as that reflected from a white wall, is sufficient to keep them healthy. A combination of equal parts of sharp sand and commercial potting soil is a good mixture for all crassulas. These succulents require temperatures between 68° and 72° during the day and between 50° and 55° at night. Keep them fairly dry and cool during winter dormancy. During their growth period in spring and summer, keep the soil moist at all times by watering liberally, so water runs out of the pot into the saucer. Empty the saucer after watering so roots do not rot. Feed weekly in spring and summer with a solution of high-phosphorus fertilizer, such as 15-30-15, diluted to one fourth the recommended strength. Repot when necessary at any season, although crassulas do best crowded in their pots. Propagate at any time from stem or leaf cuttings. Outdoors, crassulas will grow in Zone 10.

CRESTED EUPHORBIA See *Euphorbia*
CROCODILE-JAWS See *Aloe*
CROWN, SILVER See *Cotyledon*
CROWN CACTUS See *Rebutia*
CROWN-OF-THORNS See *Euphorbia*
CRYOPHYTUM See *Mesembryanthemum*

D

DAISY, LIVINGSTON See *Mesembryanthemum*
DANCING BONES See *Hatiora*
DESERT ROSE See *Adenium* and *Mesembryanthemum*
DEVIL'S BACKBONE See *Pedilanthus*
DOLLAR, SAND See *Astrophytum*
DONKEY'S TAIL See *Sedum*
DOROTHEANTHUS See *Mesembryanthemum*
DROSANTHEMUM See *Mesembryanthemum*
DRUNKARD'S DREAM See *Hatiora*
DUTCHMAN'S-PIPE CACTUS See *Epiphyllum*

E

EASTER CACTUS See *Schlumbergera*
EASTER LILY CACTUS See *Echinopsis*

ECHEVERIA
E. agavoides (wax agave); *E. derenbergii* (painted lady); *E. elegans,* also called *Cotyledon elegans* (Mexican snowball); *E.* hybrid 'Ballerina'; *E. peacockii,* also called *E. desmetiana* (peacock echeveria)
Size: 2 to 9 inches in diameter

Growing wild from Texas to Argentina, ground-hugging, succulent echeverias often bear leaves in decorative rosettes suitable either for potting or, in warm regions, for use in rock gardens and flower beds. Species vary widely in form and texture, and some occasionally send up slender stalks bearing bell-shaped flowers in small clusters at the tips. The leaves of wax agave are triangular, fleshy and set in close green rosettes with red margins. Painted lady has pale green-gray leaves often rimmed with red; flower stalks emerge from between the leaves and produce clusters of orange flowers.

Mexican snowball appears almost alabaster because of the white, waxy protective powder covering its leaves. The hybrid Ballerina has an almost floral grace, the scalloped leaves

NECKLACE VINE
Crassula perforata

WAX AGAVE
Echeveria agavoides

For climate zones, see map, page 150.

Echeveria hybrid 'Ballerina'

growing from a narrow base and shading from gray-blue to rose as they unfold to reveal broad wavy margins. Peacock echeveria has short stems and leaves 2 inches long and 1¼ inches wide that are a silvery blue with red edges. The flowers are scarlet.

HOW TO GROW. Echeverias grow best with four to six hours a day of direct sunlight or very bright artificial light for 14 to 16 hours a day. But they grow fairly well in filtered sunlight or light reflected from white walls.

Indoors, provide night temperatures of 65° to 70° and day temperatures of 70° to 85° in spring and summer. In fall and winter, temperatures of 50° to 65° at night and 65° to 75° by day are needed. From spring through autumn let the soil become almost dry between thorough waterings; in winter, water plants even less, just enough to prevent shriveling.

Do not feed newly potted plants for one year; give established plants one spring feeding with a solution of a foliage house-plant fertilizer such as 10-20-10 diluted to half the strength recommended on the label. Repot overcrowded or straggly plants at any season; otherwise, repot in spring. Use a mixture of 1 part sharp sand and 1 part commercial potting soil, adding 1 tablespoon each of ground limestone and 1 of bone meal for every gallon of mix. Propagate plants, preferably in spring, from offsets, which are easily detached, or by stem or leaf cuttings. Echeverias will grow well outdoors in summer, but must be protected from frost except in Zone 10.

ECHINOCACTUS
E. grusonii (golden barrel cactus); *E. ingens* (large barrel cactus)
Size: 6 inches to 4 feet in diameter

In the deserts of Mexico and the southwest United States squat *Echinocacti* bake in the heat of the desert sun. They are round or cylindrical, ribbed and heavily spined and they produce flowers in a circle around their woolly crowns. The golden barrel cactus is almost round, with 21 to 37 thick, high ribs that develop when the plant is three or four years old. Although it grows very slowly, requiring ten years to reach a 6-inch diameter, it may eventually reach a diameter of 3 feet. The body is green with arching, golden spines and the crown wool is yellow. Because the 2½-inch yellow flowers bloom only after the plant is 1 foot thick, the golden barrel cactus is grown chiefly for its shape and bright colors.

The large barrel cactus, true to its name, reaches a height and width of 4 feet. A mature plant has about 50 ribs, is blue-gray and tufted with thick brown spines. When the large barrel cactus becomes 2 feet tall, it bears small yellow flowers on its crown.

HOW TO GROW. Golden barrel and large barrel cacti need direct sunlight for six hours or more a day. Keep temperatures at 50° to 55° at night and 75° or higher during the day in the growing season; in winter, keep them from 40° to 45° at night and at 65° during the day. For both species, let the soil become nearly dry between waterings in late spring and summer, and keep them absolutely dry in winter and early spring. Feed biweekly during the growing season with a high-phosphorus fertilizer such as 15-30-15 diluted to one fourth the strength recommended on the label; withhold fertilizer during winter. Pot in a commercial mix prepared for cacti, adding 1 teaspoon of bone meal or ground limestone to each gallon of the mixture. Plant seeds in late spring or early summer. Potted plants do best outdoors in full sun in summer. They can be grown as landscape plants in Zones 9 and 10, and in Zone 8 from central Texas westward.

ECHINOCACTUS See also *Ferocactus* and *Notocactus*

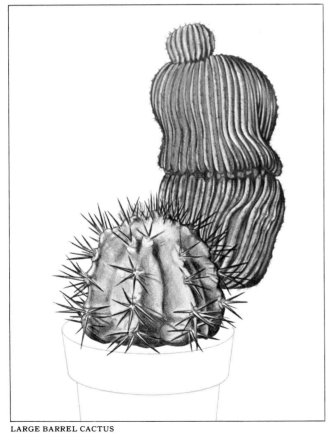

LARGE BARREL CACTUS
Echinocactus ingens

ECHINOCEREUS

E. dasyacanthus; E. engelmannii (strawberry hedgehog);
E. pectinatus (rainbow cactus)
Size: Up to 16 inches tall

Ranging widely through the western United States and Mexico, some *Echinocereus* cacti are quite hardy. Most species bloom when the plants are still small and the flowers are often spectacular. *E. dasyacanthus* is a desert plant with a cylindrical pale green stem. It is a solitary plant when young but tends to cluster as it reaches maturity. It has up to 21 ribs covered with spines varying in color from white through yellow to brown. Plants grow 9 to 16 inches tall and 3 to 4 inches thick. Likely to bloom in cultivation, it produces flowers up to 5 inches in diameter in yellow, pink and red. The strawberry hedgehog grows in sandy and rocky areas in Arizona, southern California and northern Mexico. Its stems grow up to 10 inches tall and 2 inches thick; each has 11 to 14 shallow ribs covered with sharp spines, some as long as 2 inches, colored white, yellow or pink. The plant clumps in groups of 12 or more. Flowers are purple and about 3 inches in diameter. Rainbow cactus grows in both grassland and desert regions in Mexico, eastern Arizona and western Texas. Its squat cylinders 4 to 12 inches tall are up to 4 inches thick. Heavily covered with spines, the stems have about 20 ribs, grow either singly or with two or three branches and are banded with yellow and pink stripes, pinker in young plants. At a height of 3 inches the rainbow may begin to produce scented pink flowers up to 3 inches across.

HOW TO GROW. Indoors or out, *Echinocereus* cacti need bright sunlight throughout the year, six hours a day in the growing season and four hours in winter. They do well with temperatures of 65° to 90° in summer and 45° to 55° in winter. Some species survive freezing weather when the soil is very dry. In pots, the soil should become almost dry to the touch between waterings in spring and summer and totally dry during winter dormancy. Plants should be fed monthly from spring through summer with a high-phosphorus fertilizer, such as 15-30-15, at half the strength suggested on the label. Pot plants in spring in a very porous mixture of 1 part sharp sand to 1 part commercial potting soil.

Outdoors, *Echinocereus* plants can be grown in Zones 9 and 10, and in Zone 8 from central Texas westward, with full sun and good drainage in winter. If allowed to become waterlogged, their roots die. Propagation is from seed.

ECHINOFOSSULOCACTUS

E. multicostatus, also called *Stenocactus multicostatus* (brain cactus)
Size: Up to 6 inches tall

High, thin wavy ribs, at least 100 of them, distinguish this cactus, giving a wrinkled look to its near globular shape and earning it the common name, brain cactus. It is native to the sunny mountains of Mexico. Seldom taller than 6 inches, it usually grows singly rather than in clumps. From new growth on the top of the plant, white flowers appear in summer with petals erect or partly expanded. Cultivated plants bloom readily, but they must be at least three years old. Ribs each have one or two areoles with broad, sharp yellow spines, ½ to 3 inches long.

HOW TO GROW. As an indoor plant, brain cactus must have bright light all year long, six hours a day in summer and four hours a day in winter. It grows best with temperatures of 65° to 90° in spring and summer and 45° to 55° in winter. In spring and summer, let the soil in the container become dry to the touch before watering thoroughly; give brain cactus a cool, dry winter, watering only after the soil has be-

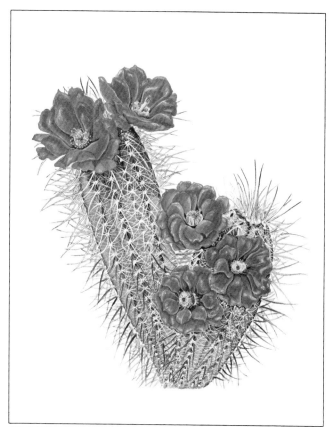

STRAWBERRY HEDGEHOG
Echinocereus engelmannii

RAINBOW CACTUS
Echinocereus pectinatus

For climate zones, see map, page 150.

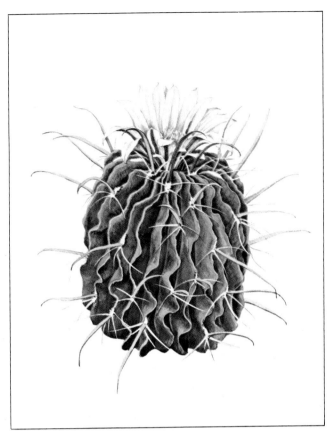

BRAIN CACTUS
Echinofossulocactus multicostatus

come totally dry. Feed with a high-phosphorus fertilizer, such as 15-30-15, following label instructions, monthly in spring and summer. Do not feed in winter. Repot in spring in equal parts of sharp sand and commercial garden soil.

Outdoors, the brain cactus is hardy for rock-garden planting in Zones 9 and 10, and in Zone 8 from central Texas westward. Plant in sandy loam with partial shade; feed once each spring with a high-phosphorus fertilizer.

ECHINOPSIS
E. hybrid 'Haku Jo'; *E. longispina,* also called *Lobivia longispina; E. multiplex,* also called *Cereus multiplex* (Easter lily cactus)
Size: Up to 10 inches tall

Hardy plants, these cacti grow rapidly and, when they have reached a height of about 3 inches, produce beautiful, night-blooming, white-to-pink funnel-shaped flowers on long tubes. The hybrid Haku Jo produces many small globes that have deep ribs and rust-colored spines. Large pink or white blooms appear throughout the summer. Bristling with 3-inch-long needle-like spines, *E. longispina* has 25 to 50 wavy ribs wrinkling its 10-inch-tall stem. Its flowers are small, only 1½ inches long. Easter lily cactus is a 12- or 15-ribbed globe up to 8 inches high, bearing, in late spring, fragrant pink flowers 8 to 10 inches across. The areoles have 1-inch, curved, black-tipped brown spines.

HOW TO GROW. These plants grow best with four to six hours of direct sunlight each day, winter and summer, or with 12 to 14 hours of bright artificial light; but they also grow in bright indirect light, such as that reflected from white walls. Temperatures should be 65° to 70° at night and 75° to 85° by day in spring and summer; in winter, temperatures should be 40° to 55° at night and under 65° by day. Keep the soil moderately dry to the touch between thorough waterings from spring through autumn; in winter it should be kept very dry. Too much heat or water will produce large numbers of offsets but few blossoms. Newly potted plants should be left unfertilized for one year, and established plants should be fed once annually during the flowering season with a high-phosphorus fertilizer such as 15-30-15 used as directed on the label. For fast growth, repot in early spring, or remove and pot basal shoots. If these shoots have been kept dry in winter, they will survive and begin to flower when they are about 3 inches in diameter. They should be potted in a mixture of 1 part sharp sand and 1 part commercial potting soil, with 1 tablespoon each of ground limestone and of bone meal added to every gallon of mix.

Outdoors, the Easter lily cactus, given good drainage, is hardy in Zones 5 to 10; the other species can be grown in zones 8 to 10, with good drainage essential in Zone 8. The plant should be set in light, sandy loam, where it will be partially shaded during the heat of the day. In spring, the cactus should be fed once with a high-phosphorus fertilizer, following the label. Propagation is from seed.

ECHINOPSIS See also *Lobivia*
ELEPHANT BUSH See *Portulacaria*
ELEPHANT EAR See *Kalanchoe*
ELEPHANT-FOOT TREE See *Beaucarnea*
ELEPHANT TREE See *Bursera*

EPIPHYLLUM
E. ackermannii, also called *Nopalxochia ackermannii; E.* hybrid 'Paul de Longpre'; *E. oxypetalum,* also called *Phyllocactus latifrons* (queen-of-the-night, Dutchman's-pipe cactus)
Size: Trailing stems about 3 feet long

Echinopsis hybrid 'Haku Jo'

For more than 100 years, growers have been hybridizing the tree- and cliff-growing epiphytic cacti of the *Epiphyllum* genus, developing plants that are sought chiefly for their vigor and their profuse, large, colorful flowers. Many varieties bloom periodically throughout the year; the blossoms, which are often fragrant, appear on soft, waxy stems. The stems are long and twisted or flat, and they may grow to a length of 3 feet.

E. ackermannii has many 4- to 6-inch funnel-shaped crimson flowers, usually opening in daytime and blooming frequently in autumn and winter as well as in summer. The hybrid Paul de Longpre is attractively displayed in a hanging basket; its blooms are yellow and very open and are up to 6 inches in diameter. Queen-of-the-night has many large, flat, thin, waxy green branches. Some consider it the best choice of the night-blooming cacti for enhancing a home interior. Its 5-inch star-shaped flowers, which are white with a touch of red at their bases, have an intense vanilla fragrance; its branches grow to 3 feet long.

HOW TO GROW. Epiphyllums do best in bright indirect or curtain-filtered sunlight. They need spring and summer temperatures of 60° to 65° at night and 70° to 85° in the daytime. In winter, they will tolerate temperatures down to 40°, but a range of 50° to 55° is better. High night temperatures in winter cause stems to grow rather than flower buds. Pot epiphyllums in a mixture of 1 part peat moss, leaf mold or sphagnum moss and 1 part sand or gravel. Keep moist but avoid the use of alkaline water because this unusual cactus prefers acidity.

Fertilize monthly from spring through fall with a low-nitrogen house-plant fertilizer, such as 5-10-10, following the instructions on the package. Keep the planting mixture moist at all times. Omit feeding during the winter months. Propagate by cuttings taken from mature branches in spring or after flowering in summer; allow the cuttings to dry for two weeks, then place them in barely moist sand or a mixture of half sand and half perlite to root. Do not water the cuttings for three weeks, then gradually begin watering. Outdoors in summer, epiphyllums thrive in hanging baskets suspended from shade trees. The plants are very sensitive to frost and should be moved indoors early in fall.

EPITHELANTHA

E. micromeris (button cactus, golf balls)
Size: Up to 1½ inches in diameter when mature

Growing in tight clusters of 20 to 30 spheres covered with short white spines, button cacti are dwarf globes 1 to 1½ inches in diameter. Small pink flowers may project through the wool at the top of a globe in spring, though the plant does not readily flower away from its natural habitat in Texas and Mexico. The red fruit is cylindrical, about ½ inch long. Button cacti grow very slowly, but since they cluster freely, they can be easily propagated.

HOW TO GROW. Button cacti need four or more hours of direct sunlight daily, all year long. They grow best with spring and summer temperatures of 65° to 90°, and fall and winter temperatures of 45° to 55°. They must have low humidity and a coarse, well-drained soil such as a mixture of 2 parts sharp sand with 1 part commercial potting soil. Since button cacti grow on limestone hills in Texas and northern Mexico, the addition of a powdered lime to the potting mixture is helpful. Judicious watering is in order: during the spring and summer growing season, let the soil become almost dry before watering sparingly; in fall and winter, water just enough to keep the plant from shriveling. One tablespoon of water weekly for a plant in a 4-inch pot should be

Echinopsis longispina

Epiphyllum hybrid 'Paul de Longpre'

For climate zones, see map, page 150.

BUTTON CACTUS
Epithelantha micromeris

PERUVIAN OLD-MAN CACTUS
Espostoa lanata

sufficient during the growing season, with perhaps a light misting to simulate natural dew.

Feed button cacti monthly during the spring and summer months with a high-phosphorus fertilizer, such as 15-30-15, diluted to half the strength that is recommended on the label; do not feed in winter. If a cluster spreads to the edge of its pot, repot in spring or break off the small new growths and root them separately.

ESPOSTOA

E. lanata (Peruvian old-man cactus, snowball cactus)
Size: Up to 3 feet when mature

Densely covered with fine white hairs that are silky when new, the Peruvian old-man cactus grows as a column, sometimes branching near the top. A plant 6 inches tall can be expected to grow 1½ to 2 inches a year, eventually reaching about 3 feet. This cactus rarely blooms in cultivation.

HOW TO GROW. Because dense hairs screen its stem, Peruvian old-man cactus must have very bright light all year in order to thrive. Indoors, give it four to six hours of direct sunlight or 12 to 14 hours of strong artificial light daily. Keep temperatures between 65° and 90° in spring and summer, and between 45° and 55° in autumn and winter. Let the soil become dry to the touch, then water thoroughly in spring and summer and do not water during dormancy. Moisture in winter can cause rot at the base. Feed monthly from spring through autumn with a solution of high-phosphorus fertilizer such as 15-30-15; do not feed at all during winter. Repot when necessary in spring in a mixture of 1 part sharp sand and 1 part commercial potting soil. Propagate from seed. If hairs on the lower stem begin to darken and fall, giving the plant a shopworn appearance, cut off the top, dry it thoroughly and set it in damp vermiculite or sand to root.

EUPHORBIA

E. antisyphilitica (candelilla); *E. grandicornis* (cow's horn); *E. lactea* (milk-striped euphorbia); *E. lactea cristata* (crested euphorbia); *E. milii splendens,* also called *E. splendens* (crown-of-thorns); *E. obesa* (basketball euphorbia, living baseball, gingham golf ball)
Size: 2 inches to 20 feet tall

About 1,500 kinds of euphorbias grow wild throughout the world and vary tremendously in appearance. Some of them are thorny, some have no thorns. Many succulent euphorbias from Africa and Asia resemble cacti except for the absence of areoles. A number of euphorbias exude both a fine mist and, when they are cut, a milky sap that can be irritating to eyes and cause a skin rash.

Candelilla is an olive-green spineless plant with leafless, slender stems rising to a height of 3 feet. In early spring it produces five white bracts, modified leaves that resemble a single flower. The cow's horn has succulent branches that rise in constricted segments, gnarled, twisted and bristling with spines up to 2½ inches long. This shrub grows up to 3 feet tall. The small flowers are yellow. Milk-striped euphorbia looks like a green candelabra. It grows 10 feet tall or more and has leafless triangular or square stems that are streaked with white and lined along the ridges with pairs of spines. The leaves and flowers are very inconspicuous. Crested euphorbia is a spiny shrub with dark green crumpled stems. It can be used as a hedge, growing 10 to 20 feet high over many years.

The crown-of-thorns is a branching, very spiny plant that grows up to 3 feet tall. The branches, ⅜ inch thick, have numerous ¾-inch spines. Green leaves up to 2 inches long drop off as the plant ages. Small red, rose, salmon or yellow blossoms bloom at the tips of the branches. If it is kept moist, crown-of-thorns flowers throughout the year. Basketball euphorbia is a succulent gray-green globe with fine purple striping and usually eight spineless ridges that look like stitching. With age, the globe may lengthen, growing into an elongated sphere 8 inches tall and 3½ inches wide.

Euphorbias are usually grown as potted house plants, but they make dramatic landscaping plants in the subtropical areas where they will survive the winters.

HOW TO GROW. Indoors, euphorbias thrive in four or more hours of filtered sunlight or 12 to 16 hours of artificial light daily, but will grow fairly well with bright indirect light such as that reflected from white walls. Night temperatures of 55° to 65° and day temperatures of 70° to 80° are ideal. Let the soil of most euphorbias become dry to the touch between thorough waterings. Cow's horn and crown-of-thorns should be protected from drafts and may need richer soil and more moisture than other euphorbias to keep the leaves from dropping. The soil of the basketball cactus should be allowed to dry completely between waterings, since it is very subject to rot. For most euphorbias, plant in a mixture of equal parts sharp sand and commercial potting soil, with 1 tablespoon of ground limestone and 1 tablespoon of bone meal added to each gallon of mix. If light is good, fertilize monthly in summer with a balanced house-plant fertilizer, such as 10-10-10, diluted to half strength; if light is but moderate, feed only once at the beginning of summer.

Propagate basketball euphorbia at any season from seeds. New plants of other species can be started in spring and summer from stem cuttings. Swab both the cuttings and the plants from which they were taken with cold water, and allow the cuttings to heal as long as necessary to form calluses—from several days to a week, depending on the size of the parent plant. Put the cuttings into sand until they set roots, keeping the sand slightly moist. When roots form, usually after a few weeks, repot them. Dry crown-of-thorns cuttings for only one day, rather than several, and keep their sand moist while they form roots. Grown outdoors, cow's horn and crown-of-thorns are hardy in Zone 10.

F

FAIRY WASHBOARD See *Haworthia*

FAUCARIA

F. tigrina, also called *Mesembryanthemum tigrina* (tiger jaws); *F. tuberculosa,* also called *Mesembryanthemum tuberculosum*

Size: 4 to 6 inches tall

These dwarf, almost stemless succulents from southern Africa have fierce-looking but soft teeth along the edges of their dark green three-sided leaves. On young growth the teeth interlock; later the leaves open like menacing, gaping jaws. The large yellow flowers bloom in early spring, generally opening in the afternoon, then closing until the following afternoon. Flowering usually begins in the second year and individual blossoms may last for several days. The tiger jaws' rigid leaves are 1 inch wide at the base and taper 1½ to 2 inches to a point. Each leaf has nine or 10 teeth and white markings. The 2-inch-wide flowers sometime appear in pairs. The thick, short leaves of *F. tuberculosa* are 1 inch long and ¾ inch wide; from above they appear triangular. Three stout teeth appear on the edges and tiny white tubercules, like emerging baby teeth, grow on the upper surfaces. The yellow flower is 1½ inches wide.

HOW TO GROW. In their native habitat, these plants grow in winter and are dormant in summer; in cultivation in the

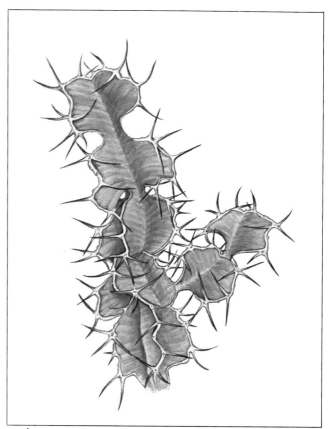

COW'S HORN
Euphorbia grandicornis

BASKETBALL EUPHORBIA
Euphorbia obesa

For climate zones, see map, page 150.

TIGER JAWS
Faucaria tigrina

FISHHOOK
Ferocactus acanthodes

Northern Hemisphere they may adapt to the usual summer-growth schedule. Both species grow best in bright light, four to six hours of direct sun or 12 to 14 hours of strong artificial light daily in the growing season. Temperatures between 65° and 90° are needed for active growth; during dormancy the plants will tolerate temperatures as low as 50°. They require a very porous soil such as a mixture of 2 parts sharp sand and 1 part commercial potting soil. While a plant is in active growth, let the soil become dry to the touch before watering; water less frequently when it is dormant. Feed monthly during the growing season with a high-phosphorus fertilizer such as 15-30-15, diluted to half the strength recommended on the label; do not feed during dormancy. Propagate from seed, or by dividing a clump when repotting. Faucarias can be grown outdoors in Zones 9 and 10.

FEATHER CACTUS See *Mammillaria*
FENESTRARIA See *Mesembryanthemum*

FEROCACTUS
F. acanthodes, also called *Echinocactus acanthodes* (fishhook, visnaga, barrel cactus); *F. townsendianus*
Size: Up to 10 feet tall

These cacti have fierce, often beautifully colored spines on stems that are globular, oval or cylindrical in shape. Their ribs are formed of almost adjoining projections with areoles producing more than 20 spines each. In their native habitats—California, Texas and Mexico—they grow 10 feet high and 2 feet thick, but this growth takes many years. These cacti bloom when they reach 1 foot in height; flowers are 1½ to 3 inches wide and bell- or funnel-shaped, appearing in spring at the top of the stem. In nature, fishhook is a column 6 to 10 feet tall and 1 foot thick, with 16 to 28 ribs, but a 5-inch-tall house plant will grow no more than 1 inch in two years. Spines are pink to brilliant red, often twisted and hooked; flowers are orange or yellow. *F. townsendianus* is a 16-inch-tall cylinder with long, slender spines and orange flowers. These cacti grow so slowly that seedlings serve well as colorful window-sill plants.

HOW TO GROW. To keep a pleasing shape, these cacti need as much sunlight as possible all year. Keep spring and summer temperatures between 65° and 90° and fall and winter temperatures between 45° and 55°. Plant in a mixture of 1 part sharp sand and 1 part commercial potting soil. In the spring and summer growth season, let the soil become dry to the touch between waterings; keep the plants very dry in fall and winter. Feed every two months from spring to fall with a solution of a balanced house-plant fertilizer, such as 10-10-10, diluted as directed on the label. Do not feed in winter.

Outdoors, these cacti can be grown in Zones 9 and 10 and in Zone 8 from central Texas west. Set the plants in full sun outdoors in summer if possible, but keep them at some distance from walkways; spines and passersby can damage each other. Feed once each spring with a sprinkling of bone meal. Propagate from seeds.

FIG, HOTTENTOT See *Mesembryanthemum*
FISHHOOK See *Ferocactus*
FLAME, BLUE See *Myrtillocactus*

FOUQUIERA
F. columnaris, also called *Idria columnaris* (boojum tree); *F. fasciculata; F. purpusii*
Size: Up to 40 feet tall outdoors

These curious, spiny semisucculent shrubs grow over a wide area of southwestern United States and northern Mexico. In their natural habitat fouquieras sometimes grow to a height of 30 to 40 feet. The leaves grow either clustered or nearly solitary; blossoms are showy in some species and often insignificant in others.

Boojum tree's swollen, pulpy trunk is shaped like an inverted cone; spiraling gray-green spiny branches grow near the top. It bears sprays of creamy small blossoms that look somewhat like babies'-breath. Both *F. fasciculata* and *F. purpusii* also have cone-shaped bases which are scaly and woody and are marked with subtle shadings of green and deep red. Moss will occasionally grow on the bases. As house plants they grow very slowly. A cone that is 15 inches tall may be 15 years old, an 18-inch cone 20 years old. The branches, however, grow several feet each year, and should be clipped back while the plants are in active growth to give them a pleasing shape.

HOW TO GROW. Indoors, give fouquieras four to six hours of direct sunlight or 16 hours of strong artificial light daily all year. Keep temperatures between 50° to 75°. While plants are growing actively in spring and summer, let the soil become dry to the touch between waterings; in fall and winter let it dry completely, watering only enough to keep the plants from shriveling. Feed every two months during the growing season with a foliage-house-plant fertilizer, such as 10-20-10, diluted to half the strength recommended on the label. Repot fouquieras in spring, using a mixture of 2 parts sharp sand and 1 part commercial potting soil. Propagate from seeds or cuttings.

Outdoors, fouquieras are hardy in Zones 9 and 10 and in Zone 8 from central Texas westward. They grow best in sandy, alkaline soil. When preparing a bed for young plants, work a small amount of loam into the soil. Mature plants need full sun; provide partial shade for young plants during the heat of the day. Fertilize the plants each spring with foliage-plant fertilizer.

G

GASTERIA
G. caespitosa (pencil leaf); *G. liliputana* (Lilliput gasteria)
Size: 2 to 6 inches tall without flower stalks

Vigorous and easy to grow, gasterias are stemless succulents with interesting markings on their 2- to 14-inch fleshy leaves. These sometimes grow in rosettes, but usually they rise from the base of each plant, then separate into facing rows. Pencil leaf has smooth, slim, triangular green leaves up to 5½ inches long and ¾ inch wide, their upper surfaces spotted with lighter green dots. The 2-inch-high Lilliput gasteria forms clumps and bears shiny dark green leaves about 2 inches long and an inch wide covered with white.

HOW TO GROW. Gasterias need little coddling as house plants and will grow even in a north-facing window, although they do best in bright indirect or curtain-filtered sunlight. In winter, give them night temperatures of 50° to 55° and day temperatures of 55° to 70°. Give them night temperatures of 55° to 70° and day temperatures of 70° to 85° in summer. Plant in an equal mixture of sharp sand and commercial potting soil, with 1 tablespoon of ground limestone and 1 tablespoon of bone meal added to each gallon of the mix. Let the soil become almost dry between waterings. Feed gasterias every two months through spring and summer with a balanced house-plant fertilizer, such as 10-10-10, diluted to half the strength recommended on the label; do not feed the plants in fall and winter. Repot plants that are overcrowded at any season. Propagate gasterias at any season, but preferably in spring, from seeds, leaf cuttings or the young shoots at the base of a plant.

For climate zones, see map, page 150.

Fouquiera fasciculata

Gasteria liliputana

Greenovia aurea

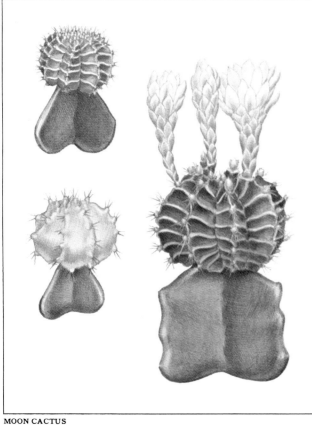

MOON CACTUS
Gymnocalycium graft

GREENOVIA

G. aurea, also called *Sempervivum aureum*

Size: Rosettes 1 to 5 inches in diameter

This succulent plant, grown indoors in the United States, is native to the mountains of the Canary Islands. In dormancy it forms clumps of cuplike rosettes; in the growing season the rosettes greatly expand, sending up leafy flower stalks 6 to 18 inches high. Greenovia rosettes are 2 to 5 inches wide with leaves 2 to 4 inches long. They are salmon colored in dormancy and blue-green during the growing season. Early in spring, flower stalks covered with clasping leaves rise up to 18 inches high and bear clusters of yellow flowers. When the flower heads die, offsets occasionally grow on horizontal stems from the base of the plant.

HOW TO GROW. Indoors, greenovias grow best in moderate, filtered light, with year-round temperatures of 65° to 90°. The dormant greenovia has been known to withstand colder temperatures if kept quite dry. Its natural growing period occurs in winter, but plants being cultivated often switch over to a late spring growth schedule. In the dormant season, the soil should be quite dry; when the rosettes are open, the soil should become dry to the touch between liberal waterings. While a plant is growing it requires monthly feeding with a high-phosphorus fertilizer, such as 15-30-15, diluted to half strength; in dormancy it needs no fertilizer. Propagate by planting the small rosettes produced during the growing season in a mixture of equal parts of sharp sand and commercial potting soil, adding 1 tablespoon of ground limestone and 1 tablespoon of bone meal to the mixture.

GYMNOCALYCIUM

G. denudatum (spider cactus); *G. mihanovichii* (plaid cactus, chin cactus); *G. quehlianum*

Size: 1 to 4 inches tall, 2 to 6 inches in diameter when mature

Its smooth naked flower buds and tubes distinguish this cactus. When not in bud, the small globular plants can be recognized by their chins, individual clefts below protuberances beneath the areoles. These cacti bloom readily indoors in spring, producing white, pink or occasionally yellow flowers, up to 3 inches across, in succession over a period of several days; some species continue to flower through autumn. Spider cactus is a green plant with ½-inch yellow spines that sprout, spider-like, along five to eight low, rounded ribs. The flowers, up to 3 inches across, range in color from white to pale rose. Plaid cactus has faint red bands that mark its gray-green body and gray ⅜-inch curved spines. Freely blooming, the plant produces pale yellow-green flowers tinged with pink. The plaid cactus and its mutant forms are commonly joined with a flat graft to hylocereus stock to form what is popularly known as the moon cactus. *G. quehlianum* is green with ivory-colored spines that redden at the base. Its white flowers have red-tinted centers and appear on the juvenile form as well as on mature specimens.

HOW TO GROW. Gymnocalyciums grow best under at least four hours of direct sunlight daily; they also do fairly well in bright indirect light, except for grafted varieties, which need bright light to hold their colors. They require year-round night temperatures of 50° to 55° and day temperatures of 68° to 72°. In winter, water just enough to keep the plant from shriveling; allow soil to dry thoroughly between waterings from spring through autumn, watering only when the top of the soil in the container feels dry to the touch. Fertilize annually each spring with a high-phosphorus fertilizer such as 15-30-15, following label instructions; do not fertilize newly potted plants the first year. Pot in equal parts of sharp sand and commercial potting soil, adding 1 tablespoon of ground limestone and 1 tablespoon of bone meal to each gallon of mix. Repot in any season when plants become overcrowded. Propagate by seed at any time of the year; propagate colored varieties in spring by grafting plantlets that may develop around the base or sides of the plant to a green cactus stock such as *Hylocereus* or *Myrtillocactus.*

H

HAHN'S SANSEVIERIA See *Sansevieria*

HARRISIA
H. martinii
Size: Stems 6 feet long or more

Harrisias sprawl thicket-like in their native South America. Their tall slender stems, erect when young, bend and grow along the ground as they mature, branching and flowering. Needle-shaped spines spring from their broad ribs. *H. martinii,* a particularly vigorous species, has nearly cylindrical stems about an inch thick. The areoles bear gray wool, short radial spines and a long central spine; stems tend to become spineless with age. Eight-inch-long white nocturnal flowers are followed by spiny, gray-tufted red seed pods 1½ inches in diameter. The plant makes good grafting stock and it can be trained to climb walls.

HOW TO GROW. Harrisias require at least four hours of direct sunlight daily to flower profusely, but will also grow well—though they may not flower—in bright indirect light. Winter temperatures of 40° to 45° at night and 65° in the daytime are ideal; from spring through autumn, harrisias need temperatures of 65° to 70° at night and 75° to 85° by day. During winter, allow soil to dry thoroughly between waterings; from spring through autumn, water when the top layer of soil in the container is dry. Use a high-phosphorus water-soluble chemical fertilizer, such as 15-30-15, annually in spring but leave newly potted plants unfertilized for the first year. Dilute the fertilizer as recommended on the label. Pot in equal parts sharp sand and commercial potting soil, adding 1 tablespoon of ground limestone and 1 tablespoon of bone meal to each gallon of mix. Propagate at any season from plantlets at the base of established plants or from seed. Outdoors, harrisia is hardy in Zone 10.

HATIORA
H. salicornioides (dancing bones, drunkard's dream)
Size: Stems 8 inches to 2 feet long

Its thin, bottle-shaped jointed stems give this cactus one of its nicknames—drunkard's dream. The stems of this tree-dweller are erect when young but become pendant as they grow, sometimes reaching 6 feet in length in the wild. The

Gymnocalycium quehlianum

Harrisia martinii

For climate zones, see map, page 150.

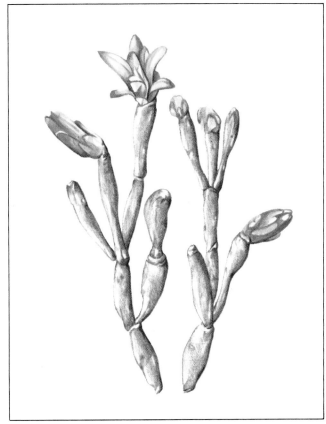

DANCING BONES
Hatiora salicornioides

FAIRY WASHBOARD
Haworthia limifolia

plant blooms in late winter, producing ⅜-inch-long yellow, orange or salmon-colored flowers on the tip of each stem. This cactus is commonly planted in a hanging basket where the stems can cascade freely.

HOW TO GROW. Dancing bones grows well in bright indirect sunlight. Spring through autumn, it does best with night temperatures of 65° to 70° and day temperatures of 75° to 85°. In winter, it requires night temperatures of 45° to 55° and day temperatures no higher than 65°. Water thoroughly, even in winter, when the top layer of soil feels dry to the touch, since extreme dryness at the roots can cause stem joints to drop off. During active growth, fertilize every six weeks with a foliage-plant fertilizer such as 5-10-5, following label instructions. Pot in equal parts commercial potting soil and sharp sand. Add 1 tablespoon of ground limestone and 1 tablespoon of bone meal to each gallon of soil mix. Propagate in early spring by rooting stem cuttings.

HAWORTHIA

H. cymbiformis (window plant); *H. fasciata* (zebra haworthia); *H. limifolia* (fairy washboard); *H. reinwardtii* (wart plant)
Size: 1½ to 6 inches tall

Succulent haworthias are valued for their fascinating leaf formations and unusual markings. They are small plants, with gray, brown or green leaves often dotted with warty protuberances called tubercles. All haworthias produce insignificant flowers. The window plant is stemless, with 1½-inch-long oval leaves that are blue-green with dark vertical stripes. The tips of the leaves are translucent, hence its name. Fairy washboard resembles the window plant in size but has triangular dark green leaves. Its leaf surfaces have numerous horizontal ribs. The zebra haworthia is the best-known species of this genus. It forms a stemless rosette 3 to 4 inches across. Its erect leaves, 1½ to 2 inches long, are marked on the undersides with horizontal white tubercles. The wart plant has stems that are 6 inches long with triangular leaves arranged in close spirals. Its lower leaf surfaces are more heavily marked with white tubercles than are the upper surfaces.

HOW TO GROW. Haworthias are among the few succulents that tolerate light shade. They are native to dry regions of southern Africa, where they grow under large bushes, an environment that can be simulated by curtain-filtered sunlight. Night temperatures of 50° to 55° and day temperatures of 68° to 72° are ideal. Allow the top half of the soil in the container to dry between thorough waterings. Newly potted plants should not be fertilized the first year. Feed established plants annually in early spring with foliage-house-plant fertilizer, such as 10-20-10, at the strength recommended on the label. Pot in a mixture of equal parts packaged potting soil and sharp sand. Add 1 tablespoon of bone meal to each gallon of soil mix. Haworthias are easily propagated by cutting and rooting suckers, the young shoots that appear at the bases of established plants. New plants can also be started from leaf cuttings or from seed.

HEART VINE See *Ceropegia*
HEDGEHOG, STRAWBERRY See *Echinocereus*
HEN-AND-CHICKENS See *Sempervivum*
HORN, COW'S See *Euphorbia*
HORN CACTUS, GOAT See *Astrophytum*
HOTTENTOT FIG See *Mesembryanthemum*
HOUSELEEK, COBWEB See *Sempervivum*
HOUSELEEK, COMMON See *Sempervivum*
HOUSELEEK, SPIDERWEB See *Sempervivum*

HUERNIA

H. macrocarpa; H. keniensis

Size: Up to 5 inches high

These dwarf leafless succulents, which are native to tropical and southern Africa, grow slowly but form clusters freely. Their numerous fleshy stems, usually less than 5 inches tall, can be either erect or prostrate. The stems are covered with burrlike teeth. Due to unusual and often exotically colored blossoms produced in summer, huernias are sometimes called dragon flowers. The flowers are usually borne near the base of the stems. *H. macrocarpa* bears 1-inch flowers, yellow marked with purple lines or sometimes entirely purple. *H. keniensis* has stems whose shape varies from cylindrical to five-furrowed and produces 1¼-inch deep-purple flowers.

HOW TO GROW. Huernias grow best where they receive at least four hours of filtered sunlight each day or eight to 12 hours of strong artificial light. In winter, night temperatures of 40° to 45° and day temperatures under 65° are ideal; from spring through autumn, night temperatures of 65° to 70° and day temperatures of 75° to 85° are recommended. From spring through autumn, allow the soil in the container to become dry to the touch before watering thoroughly; in winter, water only enough to prevent plants from shriveling. Do not fertilize newly potted plants during their first year; feed established plants monthly during the growing season with a balanced house-plant fertilizer such as 10-10-10, diluted to half the strength recommended on the label. When plants become overcrowded, repot huernias in equal parts of commercial potting soil and sharp sand, adding 1 tablespoon of ground limestone and 1 tablespoon of bone meal to each gallon of mix. Propagate at any season by dividing clumps or by rooting cuttings taken during the growing season.

I

ICE PLANT See *Mesembryanthemum*
ICE PLANT, ROSEA See *Mesembryanthemum*
IVY, VELDT, See *Cissus*

J

JADE PLANT See *Crassula*
JAWS, TIGER See *Faucaria*
JOSEPH'S-COAT CACTUS See *Opuntia*
JOSHUA TREE See *Yucca*

K

KALANCHOE

K. beharensis (velvet leaf, elephant ear); *K. blossfeldiana; K. fedtschenkoi* (rainbow kalanchoe)

Size: 1 to 10 feet fall

Few groups of succulents are more varied in form than kalanchoes. Some species are grown for their plush felted leaves, some for their clusters of bright winter flowers, still others for their beautifully colored leaves. Most are small enough to fit in a window garden. Velvet leaf, an exceptionally large species, is commonly used outdoors as a shrub because it reaches a height of 3 to 10 feet. Its feltlike, irregularly shaped leaves crowded at the branch tips range from 4 to 15 inches long and 3 to 14 inches wide. They are covered with fine brown fuzz above and green felt below, hence the name. Clusters of yellowish urn-shaped flowers are borne on 10-inch stems. *K. blossfeldiana* branches symmetrically to form a rounded dome up to a foot high. It has waxy green leaves, 1 to 3 inches long, which are almost hidden when dense clusters of scarlet flowers are produced from the upper leaf axils. These kalanchoes are commonly sold in full bloom around the Christmas season. Hybrids of this species

Huernia macrocarpa

VELVET LEAF
Kalanchoe beharensis

For climate zones, see map, page 150.

RAINBOW KALANCHOE
Kalanchoe fedtschenkoi

STRING-OF-BEADS
Kleinia rowleyanus

are available with yellow, orange or salmon-colored flowers.

Rainbow kalanchoe, a bushy species, bears 1-inch, blue-green leaves with notched rose-tinged margins. Its drooping stems (as long as 2 feet) make it an attractive hanging-basket plant. In winter, it bears apricot-colored tubular flowers.

HOW TO GROW. Kalanchoes, which are hardy outdoors in Zone 10, require at least four hours of direct sunlight daily in order to flower profusely and retain their foliage colors. Ideal temperatures are 50° to 60° at night and 68° to 72° in daytime. Allow the top layer of soil to become dry before watering thoroughly. Feed kalanchoes every two weeks from May until they bloom, then withhold fertilizer until active growth resumes. Use a high-phosphorus water-soluble chemical fertilizer such as 15-30-15 diluted to half strength. When the plants become crowded, repot them in equal parts of commercial potting soil and sand. To bloom for Christmas, *K. blossfeldiana* requires at least 14 hours of complete darkness and 10 hours of sunshine or artificial light each day from September through early December. After they bloom, cut the stems off below the flowers and just above the first pair of strong leaves. Propagate *K. blossfeldiana* from stem cuttings in early autumn or from seed, which if sown by January will produce blooming plants for Christmas. The other species can be grown from stem or leaf cuttings.

KAROO ROSE See *Lapidaria*

KLEINIA
K. herreianus, also called *Senecio herreianus* (gooseberry kleinia); *K. rowleyanus,* also called *Senecio rowleyanus* (string-of-beads); *K. stapeliiformis,* also called *Senecio stapeliiformis*
Size: Stems 8 inches to 3 feet long

Kleinias are succulents so diverse in appearance that it is hard to imagine some of them being related to the others. Nevertheless, they all have brushlike flowers that are usually white or red. Gooseberry kleinia has creeping stems, 1 to 2 feet long, which look like strings of little green beads. Each bead is really a leaf, ½ inch long, elliptically shaped and marked with translucent stripes and lines. The trailing stems, leaves and the flowers that cluster on 3-inch stalks make this a popular hanging-basket plant. String-of-beads resembles gooseberry kleinia except that its leaf is rounder and a bit smaller; it has only one translucent band, 1/16 inch wide. The tufts of white flowers are borne on a shorter stalk. It, too, is a good plant for pendant display.

K. stapeliiformis, a curious and beautifully colored species, has upright, many-sided green-to-purple stems ¾ inch thick, marked with silver between the angles. Along these angles are spinelike leaves ¼ inch long. This plant branches from the base and reaches a height of 10 inches. Scarlet flower clusters, 1½ inches across, appear in summer on erect stalks 6 inches long.

HOW TO GROW. Kleinias grow best where they receive about four hours of direct sunlight or 14 to 16 hours of strong artificial light daily in the growing season; however, they will grow well in bright indirect light. Reduce artificial light to 12 hours a day in winter. Night temperatures of 50° to 55° and day temperatures of 68° to 72° are ideal. For most kleinias, allow the top of the soil in their containers to become dry to the touch before watering thoroughly from spring through autumn. *K. stapeliiformis* requires even less watering. In winter, water kleinia plants only enough to prevent them from shriveling.

Do not fertilize newly potted plants the first year, but feed established plants monthly in spring and summer with a foliage-house-plant fertilizer such as 10-20-10, following the instructions given on the label. Repot when necessary in a mixture of equal parts of commercial potting soil and sharp sand. Add 1 tablespoon of ground limestone and 1 tablespoon of bone meal to each gallon of mix. Propagate kleinias at any season by division or stem cuttings.

L

LACE ALOE See *Aloe*
LADY, PAINTED See *Echeveria*
LAMB'S-TAIL CACTUS See *Wilcoxia*
LAMPRANTHUS See *Mesembryanthemum*

LAPIDARIA
L. margaretae (Karoo rose)
Size: Up to 1¾ inches tall

Since this African succulent is not known to grow in the Karoo region of southern Africa, it is more aptly described by its generic name, *Lapidaria,* which means a group of stones, than by its common name, Karoo rose. The species has sharply chiseled blue-gray leaves, ¾ inch long, ⅜ inch wide and ⅝ inch thick, which are tinged with pink and resemble finely polished stones. The leaves usually occur in pairs united at the base; these split apart to expose a second pair of leaves. Yellow flowers about 2 inches across are produced singly from between the leaves and almost hide the plant. They bloom in October and November.

HOW TO GROW. This plant needs all the light it can get to produce its unusual leaf colors and flowers. Place it on a sunny window sill that faces south or 4 inches below the center of fluorescent tubes turned on for 16 hours daily. It grows best in temperatures above 50°. From spring until autumn, water thoroughly when the soil feels dry to the touch. After the plant flowers, water only enough to prevent shriveling. The plant may produce a second flower within a month after the first if watered well during the flowering period. Keep the plant away from high humidity; do not place it with plants that are watered frequently. Using a pot 2½ inches in diameter, plant in equal parts of commercial potting soil and sharp sand, with a half-inch layer of pea gravel in the bottom of the container. In repotting, be sure that the undersides of the leaves are above the soil line. Propagate by seed sown in autumn.

LARGE BARREL CACTUS See *Echinocactus*
LEAF, VELVET See *Kalanchoe*
LEAFY CACTUS See *Pereskia*
LEDBOURIA See *Scilla*

LEMAIREOCEREUS
L. thurberi (organ-pipe cactus)
Size: To 20 feet tall, with stems to 8 inches in diameter

Many people visualize the organ pipe when they think of cacti. This large handsome plant is native to Arizona and Mexico. Its green-to-gray stems branch freely just above the ground. Each stem has 12 to 17 ribs armed with glossy gray, brown or black spines that project from brown feltlike areoles. White to purplish nocturnal flowers, up to 3 inches long, bloom throughout May and June, followed by edible red fruit. Because of its size, the mature organ pipe is best suited to outdoor cultivation. However, seedlings grow very slowly and can be kept as window-sill plants for years.

HOW TO GROW. The organ pipe grows best where it receives at least four hours of direct sunlight each day; in bright indirect light, it will live but grow more slowly. In spring and summer, night temperatures of 60° to 65° and day

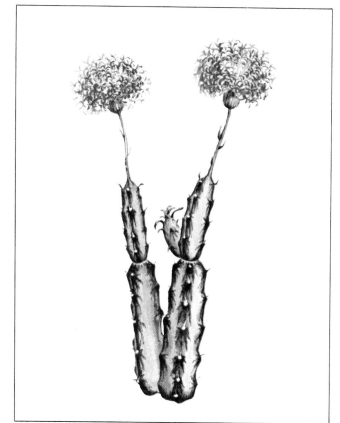

Kleinia stapeliiformis

KAROO ROSE
Lapidaria margaretae

For climate zones, see map, page 150.

ORGAN-PIPE CACTUS
Lemaireocereus thurberi

AGAVE CACTUS
Leuchtenbergia principis

temperatures of 75° to 90° are ideal. In winter, when the plant is dormant, night temperatures of 45° to 55° and day temperatures under 65° are recommended.

Indoors, during the growing season, allow soil to become dry, then water thoroughly. In winter, water only enough to prevent the plant from shriveling. Established plants should be fed once each spring with a high-phosphorus fertilizer, such as 15-30-15, following label instructions; do not feed potted plants the first year. When the plants become overcrowded, repot in equal parts of commercial potting soil and sharp sand. Add 1 tablespoon of ground limestone and 1 tablespoon of bone meal to each gallon of mix.

Outdoors, the organ pipe is hardy in Zones 9 and 10 and in Zone 8 from central Texas westward. It needs fast-draining alkaline soil. In winter, the plant can withstand light frost if the surrounding soil is not allowed to accumulate moisture. If a growing tip is damaged by frost, the cactus may produce as many as three new branches below the affected tip. Propagate at any season from seed or from small plantlets that may develop at the bases of established plants.

LEMON VINE See *Pereskia*

LEUCHTENBERGIA
L. principis (agave cactus, prism cactus)
Size: 6 to 12 inches tall

Agave cactus is curiously shaped and often mistaken for the true agave. It has turnip-like roots, a short stem and triangular tubercles up to 5 inches long and ½ to ¾ inch wide. The tubercles are blue-green in color; their blunt tips produce flat, straw-colored spines that can grow as long as 6 inches. After several years of cultivation, silky lemon-yellow fragrant flowers up to 4 inches wide emerge near the tips of young tubercles close to the center of the plant.

HOW TO GROW. The agave cactus does best with at least four hours of direct sunlight daily. For strong growth in spring and summer, it requires day temperatures of 75° to 85°, night temperatures of 60° to 65°. In winter, when it is dormant, the plant should be kept cool, with night temperatures under 65°. Allow soil to dry between waterings in spring and summer; in winter, water only enough to prevent the plant from shriveling. Newly potted plants should not be fertilized the first year; established plants should be fertilized once each spring with a foliage-house-plant fertilizer such as 10-20-10. When the plants become overcrowded, repot in 2 parts of commercial potting soil to 1 part sharp sand. Add 1 tablespoon of ground limestone and 1 tablespoon of bone meal to each gallon of mix. Agave cacti have long tap roots and grow best in deep pots. Propagate any time from seed, offshoots or tubercles, which will root in moist sand.

LINK PLANT See *Rhipsalis*

LITHOPS
L. bromfieldii; L. divergens; L. fulviceps lactinea; L. olivacea; L. optica rubra; L. salicola; L. turbiniformis (all called living stones)
Size: ⅝ to 1¼ inches high

Looking so much like pebbles that they are difficult to spot when not in bloom, living stones are native to arid regions of southern Africa. These succulents are practically stemless, with two flat semicircular leaves, up to 3 inches across, that serve as water reservoirs. Transparent windows on the top surface of the leaves enable sunlight to reach green cells inside the plant. The leaves are separated by a narrow cleft from which a new pair of leaves arises during the growing seasons; the old pair of leaves splits apart and eventually dies. White or yellow daisy-like flowers also grow from the cleft, usually in the fall.

There are about 40 species and more than 90 varieties of these living stones. The colors and patterns of their leaves vary widely but include shades of brown, gray, beige and red. *L. bromfieldii* has yellow-brown leaf tops marked with dark red netting. It grows in clumps of four to six plants. *L. divergens* grows alone or in small clumps. It is gray-green with 1-inch yellow flowers. *L. fulviceps lactinea* has rust-brown leaf tops that are patterned with gray-green spots. It grows alone or in clumps of two to four plants and produces flowers that are yellow above, white underneath. *L. olivacea* grows in large clumps ¾ inch high. It is olive-green to brown in color, often with white islands on its leaf tops. Its flowers are bright yellow, 1¾ inches across, and whiten toward the base. *L. optica rubra* is reddish-brown with a large darker brown spot on each leaf top. It produces fragrant yellow flowers and grows in clumps of up to 30 plants. *L. salicola* is gray with a large dark green spot on each leaf top. It grows alone or in clumps of up to 20 plants and produces 1-inch white flowers. The warty leaf tops of *L. turbiniformis* are reddish-brown with dark brown netting. It grows alone or in small clumps and has bright yellow flowers 1¾ inches across.

HOW TO GROW. Lithops do best where they get four or more hours of direct sunlight daily, or supply strong artificial light for 12 hours or more a day. Lithops can withstand summer temperatures up to 120°, but in winter should be kept at a relatively cool 45° to 60°. During their two growing seasons, spring and autumn, water these plants thoroughly when the top of the soil feels dry; from November through March do not water, as the plants are absorbing moisture from dying leaves. Avoid high humidity by keeping living stones away from other plants that are watered frequently. Pot in equal parts of commercial potting soil and sharp sand on top of a ½-inch drainage layer of pea gravel. Use 2½-inch pots for a single plant, or cluster several species together in a wide pan. Propagate in autumn from seed.

LIVE-FOREVER See *Sedum*
LIVING BASEBALL See *Euphorbia*
LIVINGSTON DAISY See *Mesembryanthemum*

LOBIVIA
L. famatimensis, also called *Echinopsis famatimensis* (orange cob cactus); *L. hertrichiana*; *L. paucartambensis* (cob cactus)
Size: 3 to 6 inches tall

The genus name *Lobivia* is an anagram of Bolivia where many of the species originated, growing on mountain slopes and surviving low temperatures. They owe their popularity to their abundant flowers, easy care and small size. They are globular or short cylindrical plants that grow singly or with a central stem surrounded by tiny offsets. From June through September they bear funnel- or bell-shaped flowers as large as 4 inches across; in some species the blossoms almost hide the plants. Colors include shades of red, yellow, pink, orange, purple and white. Individual flowers usually last only one day. Orange cob cactus grows 4 to 6 inches tall and 2 inches thick. It bears straight, off-white spines about ¼ inch long and yellow-to-red flowers 1½ to 3 inches long. The green globe-shaped *L. hertrichiana* grows 4 inches in diameter and produces yellow-brown spines around a curved central spine. This species and the cob cactus both produce offsets and bear bright red flowers.

HOW TO GROW. Lobivias grow best where they receive four hours a day of direct sunlight or 12 to 14 hours of strong

Lithops olivacea

LIVING STONES
Lithops bromfieldii (bottom left), L. divergens (top left),
L. fulviceps lactinea (top right), L. optica rubra (bottom right),
L. salicola (top center), L. turbiniformis (center)

For climate zones, see map, page 150.

Lobivia hertrichiana

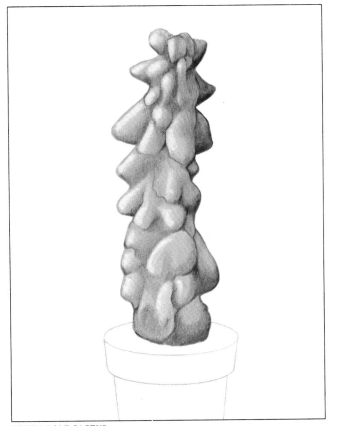

TOTEM-POLE CACTUS
Lophocereus schottii monstrosus

artificial light. In summer, however, the sun's strong rays should be curtain-filtered or they may be damaging. In winter, lobivias require night temperatures of 35° to 45° and day temperatures under 65°; a dry, cool winter is essential for flower-bud formation. From spring through fall, keep night temperatures at 65° to 70°, day temperatures at 75° to 85°.

Allow the soil to become dry to the touch before watering thoroughly during the growing season; in winter, water only enough to prevent plants from shriveling. Mist plants regularly to avoid red spider mites. Do not fertilize newly potted plants the first year, but feed established plants biweekly during the growing season with a high-phosphorous fertilizer, such as 15-30-15, diluted to one fourth the strength recommended on the label. Some species have thick, fleshy roots and should be repotted each spring; others should be repotted when they become crowded. A mix of equal parts commercial potting soil and sharp sand is suitable; add 1 tablespoon of ground limestone and 1 tablespoon of bone meal to each gallon of this mixture.

Outdoors, lobivias are hardy the year round in Zones 7-10 in regions where the humidity is low. Plant them in sandy loam where they will have good drainage, especially in winter, and provide light shade in midsummer. Propagate at any season from seed or from the offsets that develop around the bases of established plants.

LOBIVIA See also *Echinopsis*

LOPHOCEREUS
L. schottii (whisker cactus, senita); *L. schottii monstrosus* (totem-pole cactus, monstrous totem pole)
Size: To 15 feet tall when mature

The common name of the whisker cactus comes from the twisted, bristle-like gray spines, 1 to 4 inches long, borne on the upper stem. Several 1-inch nocturnal pink flowers bloom in spring and summer, followed by edible red fruits about 1 inch in diameter. Lower on the stem are short, stout gray spines less than 1/6 inch long. A native of Arizona and Mexico, whisker cactus has green, blunt-ribbed stems that branch from the base, growing to a height of 15 feet and forming clumps. Seedlings grow slowly and are attractive window-sill plants. Totem-pole cactus is essentially columnar; but because of a malformation at the growing tip, probably due to a virus, the plant appears lumpy with green knobs irregularly spaced. The ribs and most of the spines have disappeared.

HOW TO GROW. This cactus grows best where it receives at least four hours of direct sunlight each day. In winter, night temperatures of 40° to 45° and day temperatures under 65° are ideal. From spring through autumn, night temperatures of 65° to 70° and day temperatures of 75° to 85° are recommended. Outdoors, the plant can be grown in Zone 10 and in the part of Zone 9 that is in Arizona and western Texas. It requires fast-draining alkaline soil. Indoors, the top of the soil in the container should dry between thorough waterings from spring through autumn. But in winter, plants require only enough water to prevent them from shriveling. Established plants should be fertilized once each spring with a foliage-house-plant fertilizer such as 10-20-10, following label instructions. Pot in equal parts of commercial potting soil and sharp sand, adding 1 tablespoon of ground limestone and 1 tablespoon of bone meal for each gallon of mix. Propagate at any season from new plants, which may develop at the base of established plants, or from seed.

M

MALACOCARPUS See *Notocactus*

MAMMILLARIA

M. bocasana (powder-puff cactus); *M. camptotricha* (bird's-nest cactus); *M. candida* (snowball pincushion); *M. hahniana* (old-lady cactus); *M. parkinsonii* (owl eyes); *M. plumosa* (feather cactus)

Size: Up to 8 inches tall

Should a cactus fancier grow only mammillarias, he would have a never-ending source of variety and interest. They constitute a large genus of cacti, more than 150 species, with enormous differences in spines, color and growth habit. Some have a single rounded stem, others form large clusters; the stems may be covered with long white hairs, soft or stiff spines, even hooks. What is common to all mammillarias is that they have no ribs but bear protuberances on the stems with spines on their tips. Flowers, produced in spring and summer, usually form garlands around the tops of the stems. White, yellow, pink and magenta are the commonest colors. Flowers are followed by shiny red fruit that may remain on the plants for many months.

Most mammillarias flower when they are young; seed-grown plants blossom in four to five years. As window-sill plants, most are ornamental even when they are not in flower, are easy to grow and remain small. Powder puff is one of the most popular cacti. A clustering species, it has blue-green rounded or oblong stems 2 inches thick; these are covered with clusters of silky white hairs, with each cluster surrounding a yellow-to-red hooked spine. Creamy yellow flowers ¾ inch long bloom abundantly in spring, followed by 1-inch-long rosy-pink seed pods. Bird's-nest cactus has many 2-inch elongated protuberances bearing white wool and long, intertwining, often twisting yellow spines. Its creamy white flowers are small but have a limelike scent.

The snowball pincushion is one of the gems of this group. It has blue-green, flat-topped spherical stems about 3 inches thick, which are covered with tiny white spines. Pink flowers ¾ inch long appear in early summer. Old-lady cactus is a white-haired plant with a short, round muffin-shaped stem 4 inches thick. It produces offsets as it matures. This species is covered with curly, hairlike bristles as well as white spines that appear to overlap. Its violet-red flowers, ¾ inch long, open in midsummer.

Owl eyes is a large, clump-forming species with stems 6 inches tall and 3 inches thick. Neatly arranged projections bear white and prominent dark-tipped spines. Flowers ⅝ inch long are white and pink; they appear in late summer. Feather cactus looks like a white mound about 3 inches thick; individual stems are difficult to distinguish because they are so densely covered with soft white spines. Although this plant does not bloom readily, it may produce greenish-white flowers ⅝ inch long.

HOW TO GROW. Mammillarias grow best indoors where they receive at least four hours of direct sunlight each day, or at least 12 hours of strong artificial light. In winter, they require night temperatures of 40° to 50° and day temperatures under 65°; from spring through autumn, they need night temperatures of 60° to 70° and day temperatures of 75° to 85°. Let the soil become dry to the touch between waterings from spring through autumn; in the winter, water only enough to prevent plants from shriveling. Do not fertilize newly potted plants the first year; feed established plants once each spring with a high-phosphorus fertilizer such as 15-30-15 as recommended on the label. For fastest growth repot annually in early spring, otherwise only when plants become crowded. Use a mix of equal parts commercial potting soil and sharp sand with 1 tablespoon each of ground limestone and bone meal added to each gallon of mix. Propa-

BIRD'S-NEST CACTUS
Mammillaria camptotricha

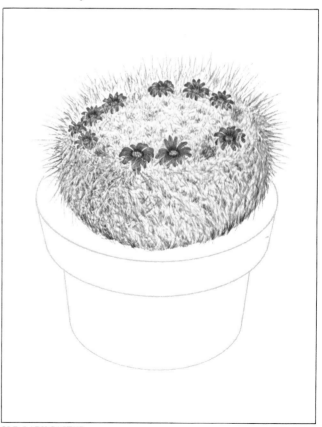

OLD-LADY CACTUS
Mammillaria hahniana

For climate zones, see map, page 150.

129

OWL EYES
Mammillaria parkinsonii

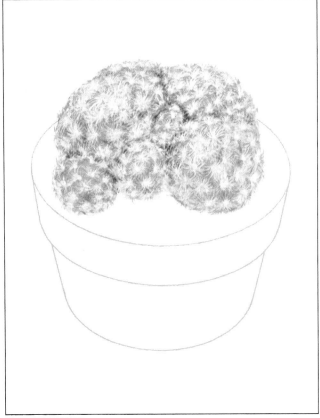

FEATHER CACTUS
Mammillaria plumosa

gate from offsets that develop at the bases of plants, or from seed. Owl eyes is planted in rock gardens in Zones 9 and 10. Give it full sun and sandy soil.

MAMMILLARIA See also *Coryphantha*

MELOCACTUS
M. intortus (Turk's cap); *M. matanzanus* (dwarf Turk's cap)
Size: 3½ inches to 3 feet tall

These distinctive plants are called Turk's caps because there is a woolly caplike structure on top of each mature plant from which flowers grow. There are about 36 species, native to tropical America and the West Indies. Globular or columnar plants, they have eight to 22 prominent ribs armed with stout spines. Small flowers that close at night are produced from the caps on mature plants. The cap, smaller in diameter than the body of the plant, bears wool and bristle-like spines, usually brown. Once it is formed the plant will not grow much larger. *M. intortus,* the larger species, grows 3 feet tall and 16 inches in diameter, with a cap 1½ feet tall and 4 inches in diameter. This species has reddish-brown spines and pink flowers ¾ inch long. The dwarf Turk's cap, a Cuban species, grows only 3½ inches tall and 4 inches thick. Creamy spines form orderly rows down its ribs. Its rosy flowers are ¾ inch long.

HOW TO GROW. Melocacti grow best indoors where they receive at least four hours of direct sunlight each day, or from 12 to 16 hours of artificial light. However, they grow fairly well in bright indirect sunlight. Year round they grow best at temperatures ranging from 65° to 90°. They are very intolerant of cold, and the temperature should never be allowed to fall below 60°, day or night. Allow the soil to become dry to the touch before watering thoroughly in the growing season; when plants are dormant, water only enough to prevent them from shriveling.

Do not fertilize newly potted plants the first year; feed established plants without caps with a foliage-house-plant fertilizer such as 10-20-10 according to the recommendations on the label once each spring. For plants with caps, use the same fertilizer but feed once every two months during the growing season. Melocacti have shallow but extensive root systems and should be repotted as soon as they become crowded, using a mixture of equal parts of commercial potting soil and sharp sand. Add 1 tablespoon of ground limestone and 1 tablespoon of bone meal to each gallon of this mixture. Propagate at any season from seed.

MESEMBRYANTHEMUM
M. criniflorum, also called *Dorotheanthus bellidiflorus, D. criniflorus, D. bellidiformus* (Livingston daisy); *M. crystallinum,* also called *Cryophytum crystallinum* (ice plant); *M. densum,* also called *Trichodiadema densum* (desert rose); *M. edule,* also called *Carpobrotus edulis* (Hottentot fig); *M. emarginatum,* also called *Lampranthus emarginatus; M. hispidum,* also called *Drosanthemum hispidum* (rosea ice plant); *M. rhopalophyllum,* also called *Fenestraria rhopalophylla* (baby toes); *M. spectabile,* also called *Lampranthus spectabilis* (trailing ice plant)
Size: 1 to 12 inches tall; trailing stems up to 3 feet long

Low-growing succulents, mostly native to arid southern Africa, the mesembryanthemums are so varied in kind that they range from bushy, woody-stemmed shrubs to tiny stemless rosettes that grow half submerged with only the tips of the plants visible. Nevertheless, almost all the mesembryanthemums flower freely, producing many-petaled daisy-like blossoms—white, yellow, pink, red and purple—that spread flat when they are open. Their fruit is usually an intricately developed seed pod that opens only in wet weather when the seeds will be most likely to germinate. The Livingston daisy is a summer-flowering annual that forms a mat about 3 inches high. Its short stems branch from a base and have rough-textured, narrow elliptical leaves 2¾ inches long and ⅜ inch wide. Variable in color, Livingston daisy's flowers open to about 1¾ inches across.

The ice plant, *M. crystallinum,* has succulent branching stems that grow prostrate to 2 feet long. Flat spoon-shaped 4-inch leaves are gray-green with a bronze cast to their tips. Covering both stems and leaves are minute projections that glisten like ice. White flowers tinted lavender, 1¼ inches across, bloom in July and August. Desert rose is a shrublike species with a fleshy root system and short, tuft-forming stems that are crowded with green leaves. These are covered with sparkling white protuberances and tipped with white bristles. In late spring to early summer red flowers, 2 inches across, appear. The creeping stems of Hottentot fig cover the ground quickly and put up thick gray-green growths of spiky three-sided leaves 3 to 5 inches long. Yellow, pink or purplish flowers up to 4 inches across appear in spring followed by edible fig-shaped fruit in midsummer.

M. emarginatum, a branched species, has thin creeping woody stems that also grow to 2 feet. Its ¾-inch leaves are powdery gray-green, slightly rough-textured and marked with translucent dots. Purple-red flowers 1¼ inches across are borne singly or in groups of three. Another creeper is the rosea ice plant. Its slender stems grow to 2 feet long and branch generously, sending up short leafy shoots and rooting rapidly. The narrow, hairy cylindrical leaves form a fine-textured mat that glistens in the sun except when the plant is covered with flowers. In late spring or early summer the foliage is covered by vivid rosy flowers an inch in diameter.

The leaves of baby toes are cylindrical, greenish-white and windowed at the top; its flowers are white and appear from October to January. The plant spreads in clumps with the leaves growing upright and curved slightly inward. In nature, baby toes grows deep in dry sand with only the blunt tips of its fat leaves exposed to gather moisture and light; in cultivation the plants are best grown with leaves well out of the soil because its higher moisture content could rot the plants. The trailing ice plant sprawls irregularly and may grow to 12 inches tall from prostrate stems, with powdery gray-olive leaves crowded on short shoots. Its flowers, growing from 3- to 6-inch stalks, are large and purple.

Baby toes and the desert rose grow best indoors. The ice plants, the Hottentot fig and the Livingston daisy are particularly useful grown outdoors in summer as ground covers in mild climates.

HOW TO GROW. Indoors these succulents grow best where they can receive at least four or more hours of bright indirect sunlight daily or at least 12 hours of strong artificial light. They need minimum temperatures of 50°, low humidity and good air circulation. Water mesembryanthemums during the growing season when the soil in their containers feels dry to the touch; otherwise water only enough to keep them from shriveling. Plant baby toes in a mixture of 2 parts sharp sand and 1 part commercial potting soil. For other species use equal parts of sand and potting soil, with 1 tablespoon of bone meal and 1 tablespoon of ground limestone added to each gallon of mix.

Outdoors the year round, ice plants are hardy on the West Coast in Zones 9 and 10; other species grow well on the West Coast in Zone 10. Provide abundant direct sunlight, with some light shade in hot climates. Mesembryanthemums grow

For climate zones, see map, page 150.

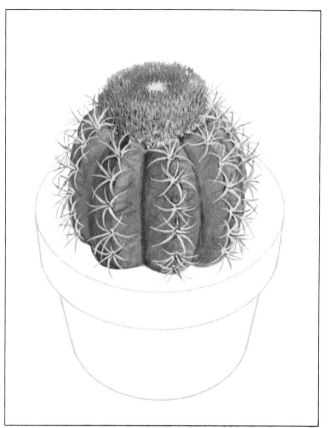

DWARF TURK'S CAP
Melocactus matanzanus

HOTTENTOT FIG
Mesembryanthemum edule

BABY TOES
Mesembryanthemum rhopalophyllum

BLUE FLAME
Myrtillocactus geometrizans

in many kinds of soil; what they require chiefly is good drainage. Set trailing plants 18 to 24 inches apart.

MESEMBRYANTHEMUM See also *Conophytum* and
   Faucaria
MEXICAN SNOWBALL See *Echeveria*
MILK-STRIPED EUPHORBIA See *Euphorbia*
MIMICRY PLANT See *Pleiospilos*
MISSOURI PINCUSHION See *Coryphantha*
MONK'S HOOD See *Astrophytum*
MONSTROUS TOTEM POLE See *Lophocereus*
MOONSTONES See *Pachyphytum*
MOTHER-OF-PEARL See *Sedum*

MYRTILLOCACTUS
M. geometrizans (blue flame)
Size: To 12 feet tall outdoors; to 5 feet as a pot plant
   A native Mexican plant, the smooth, blue-green stems of blue flame branch freely like a candelabra in the wild or when grown as an outdoor landscape plant in Zones 9 and 10 and from central Texas westward in Zone 8. Indoors, blue flame produces few branches, remains small and rarely flowers; it is grown for the unusual color of its stem, composed of five to eight prominent ribs. Pot-grown specimens have only a few spines about ½ inch long. Outdoors, white sweetly scented blossoms 1 to 1½ inches across are borne singly or in pairs. Flowers are followed by edible purple fruits that resemble raisins when dried; they are sold as delicacies in Mexican markets. The plant is a popular grafting stock.
   HOW TO GROW. The blue flame cactus requires bright light; it grows best where it receives at least four hours of direct sunlight each day. In winter, it prefers warmer temperatures than most cacti: at least 55° at night and around 65° in the daytime, although it will tolerate occasional temperatures as low as 45° in a protected area. From spring through autumn, night temperatures of 65° to 70° and day temperatures of 75° to 85° are needed. Outdoors, water the plant in hot weather only; avoid watering in winter, early spring or late autumn. Indoors, allow the top half of the soil in the container to dry between thorough waterings from spring through autumn. In winter, water only enough to prevent plants from shriveling.
   Newly potted plants should not be fertilized the first year; established plants should be fed once each spring, using an indoor foliage-house-plant fertilizer such as 10-20-10 following label instructions. Pot in equal parts of sand and commercial potting soil. Add 1 tablespoon of ground limestone and 1 tablespoon of bone meal to each gallon of mix. Propagate in spring or summer from tip cuttings or with new plants that develop at the bases of established plants or from seed.

N

NECKLACE VINE See *Crassula*
NEEDLE, ADAM'S See *Yucca*
NEEDLE PALM See *Yucca*

NEOPORTERIA
N. chilensis; N. nidus senilis
Size: 3 to 10 inches tall
   High-altitude plants native to the Andes of South America, these cacti are mostly spherical when young, but grow increasingly cylindrical. In autumn the plants bear at their tops many-petaled red, pink or yellow blossoms. *N. chilensis*, reaching a maximum height of 10 inches and a width of 4 inches, bears 2-inch-wide flowers. White or off-white spines ½ inch long ring slightly longer central spines. *N. Nidus senilis* is 3 inches high and 2½ inches thick. Densely covered

by soft, white spines up to 1¼ inches long, it bears a 3-inch-wide canopy of pink-tipped white flowers.

HOW TO GROW. These plants grow best with at least four hours of filtered sunlight a day, but they grow moderately well in bright indirect sunlight such as that reflected from light-colored walls. In winter, optimum temperatures range from between 40° and 45° at night to less than 65° during the day. From spring through fall, night temperatures of 65° to 70° and day temperatures of 75° to 85° are best. Let the top of the soil become dry to the touch between thorough waterings from spring through fall; in winter, water only enough to prevent shriveling. Do not reduce watering in autumn until growth has ceased, for these plants bloom after most cacti and continue to grow later into the fall. Newly potted plants should not be fertilized the first year; after that, feed every other month, spring through fall, with a high-phosphorus fertilizer such as 15-30-15 diluted to half the strength recommended on the label. When plants become overcrowded, repot in equal parts of commercial potting soil and sharp sand. To each gallon of this mixture add 1 tablespoon of ground limestone and 1 tablespoon of bone meal. Propagate at any season from seed.

NEST CACTUS, BIRD'S See *Thelocactus*
NIGHT-BLOOMING CEREUS See *Selenicereus*
NOBLE-STAR-FLOWER See *Stapelia*
NOPALXOCHIA See *Epiphyllum*

NOTOCACTUS

N. apricus, also called *Echinocactus apricus* (sun cup); *N. haselbergii,* also called *Malacocarpus haselbergii* (scarlet ball cactus, white-web ball cactus); *N. scopa,* also called *Echinocactus scopa* and *Malacocarpus scopa* (silver ball cactus)
Size: 3 to 5 inches tall

Native to the grasslands of South America, ball cacti are vigorous plants prized for their often colorful spines and the bright flowers produced on stems from May to July. Most are round when young but become columnar with age. Because some species flower when young, at three to five years, they are popular window-sill plants. The sun cup's pale green stem grows up to 3 inches tall indoors, its 15 to 20 ribs armed with yellow and red interlocking spines 1¼ inches long. Yellow flowers, 3 inches wide, bloom at the top of the plant. Scarlet ball cactus grows slowly up to 5 inches in diameter. It is densely covered with soft white spines, and when mature it produces long-lasting red-orange flowers ⅝ inch long. The silver ball cactus has heavily ribbed stems 4 to 5 inches tall and yellow flowers 2½ inches wide. Covering the plant, soft, white, bristle-like spines surround dark central spines.

HOW TO GROW. These cacti all grow best indoors with at least four hours of direct sunlight or 12 hours of strong artificial light each day, but they will grow fairly well in bright indirect light. In winter, night temperatures of 40° to 45° and day temperatures under 65° are ideal; from spring through autumn, night temperatures of 65° to 70° and day temperatures of 75° to 85° are recommended. In the spring and summer growing season the soil in the container should become dry to the touch between waterings. In the winter, the plants should be watered only enough to prevent shriveling. Newly potted plants should not be fed in their first year. Established plants should be fertilized biweekly in spring and summer with a high-phosphorus fertilizer, such as 15-30-15, diluted to one fourth the strength recommended on the label. Pot in equal parts of commercial potting soil and sharp sand, with 1 tablespoon of ground limestone and 1 tablespoon of bone meal added to each gallon of mix. These

Neoporteria chilensis

Neoporteria nidus senilis

For climate zones, see map, page 150.

SILVER BALL CACTUS
Notocactus scopa

plants can be propagated from seed or from the young shoots that may appear around the base of an established plant.

Outdoors, ball cacti are hardy in Zones 9 and 10 and in Zone 8 in southern Arizona if frost protection is provided. They grow best in well-drained sandy loam. Fertilize once each spring with a sprinkling of bone meal.

O

OBREGONIA

O. denegrii (artichoke cactus)
Size: 2 inches tall, up to 5 inches wide

A native of the Mexican desert, the artichoke cactus is a squat plant with leaflike wedges and spiny tips that give it a resemblance to a chunky artichoke. The small, slow-growing plant is useful in low dish gardens. Blossoming intermittently through the summer—though seldom indoors—mature plants bear flowers up to 2 inches in size on their woolly tops. Spines project from bits of floss at tips of the wedges.

HOW TO GROW. Artichoke cactus grows best with four hours or more of direct sunlight daily or 12 to 16 hours of bright artificial light. It will also grow fairly well in bright indirect light. From spring through fall, keep night temperatures between 50° and 65° and day temperatures in the 65° to 85° range; in winter, lower night temperatures by 10° and maintain day temperatures under 65°.

The soil should become dry to the touch between thorough waterings from spring through fall; in winter, water only when plants are in danger of shriveling. Newly potted plants should not be fed the first year; then they should be fed once each spring with a house-plant fertilizer used at half the strength recommended on the label or a teaspoon of bone meal sprinkled around the base of each plant. Repot in early spring when the plants become crowded. For potting, blend equal parts of commercial potting soil and sharp sand. Add 1 tablespoon of ground limestone and 1 tablespoon of bone meal to each gallon of mix. Propagate from seeds.

OCTOBER DAPHNE See *Sedum*
OCTOBER PLANT See *Sedum*
OLD-LADY CACTUS See *Mammillaria*
OLD-MAN-AND-WOMAN See *Sempervivum*
OLD-MAN CACTUS See *Cephalocereus*
OLD-MAN CACTUS, PERUVIAN See *Espostoa*
ONION, CLIMBING See *Bowiea*

OPUNTIA

O. bigelovii (teddy-bear cholla); *O. fragilis; O. humifusa,* also called *O. compressa; O. microdasys* (bunny ears); *O. paediophylla,* also called *O. glomerata, O. papyracantha* or *O. articulata diademata* (paper-spine cactus, paper cactus); *O. spinosior* (cane cholla); *O. vulgaris variegata,* also called *O. monacantha variegata* (Joseph's-coat cactus)
Size: Up to 20 feet tall

Among the best known of all cacti, these largely desert-dwelling plants include prickly pears, which have branches of fleshy, flattened pads, as well as chollas, with cylindrical stems ranging from bushy shrubs to treelike plants over three times the height of a man. The plants have no ribs, but some are heavily armored with spines, and all bear glochids—tufts of barbed bristles most painful when embedded in the skin. Brilliantly colored wheel-shaped blooms are followed by fruit, which is edible in some species and makes these plants a valuable commodity in parts of Mexico and South America.

Teddy-bear cholla, 3 to 8 feet tall with jointed, cylindrical stems 2 inches thick, is protected by stiff, silvery-yellow

ARTICHOKE CACTUS
Obregonia denegrii

spines up to 1½ inches long that become black with age. Greenish-yellow flowers 1½ inches wide bloom in the early spring, followed by yellow-green fruit. *O. fragilis,* hardy outdoors as far north as British Columbia, is a spreading 4-inch-high plant bearing bright green joints in 1- to 2-inch-long oval shapes. White, woolly areoles are surmounted by weak, 1¼-inch spines that are brown-gray or white. The plant produces green-yellow flowers in spring and summer. *O. humifusa* spreads readily, rooting from the underside of 2- to 6-inch-long joints. This plant, which has virtually no spines, bears golden-yellow flowers with red centers in early summer.

Bunny ears, one of the most familiar cacti in gardens, is a shrubby species that grows no higher than 3 feet. Its 3- to 6-inch spineless pads are not as gentle as the plant's name implies; they are covered by tufts of skin-piercing glochids. These tiny yellow bristles are set off in summer by pale yellow flowers. Paper-spine cactus grows in dense clumps of oblong joints—brown or gray-green—with 1- to 4-inch-long brown spines. The plant has reddish-brown glochids and ½-inch-wide flowers ranging from rose to yellow. Cane cholla, up to 12 feet tall with a thick main stem and long branches, is prized in Mexico, where the inner core is used for making canes. The short-spined plant bears 2-inch blossoms in a variety of colors. Its fleshy oval fruit is less than 2 inches long. Joseph's-coat cactus may reach a treelike height of 20 feet, but grows very slowly as a pot plant, maintaining a height of 1 or 2 feet for years. Flat, oval joints are 1 foot long and nearly spineless. Its yellow flowers are 3 inches wide.

HOW TO GROW. These plants grow best with at least four hours a day of direct sunlight. In winter, temperatures should range between 40° and 45° at night and less than 65° during the day; from spring through fall, raise night temperatures by 25° and keep day temperatures between 75° and 85°. Let soil become dry to the touch between thorough waterings in spring through autumn; in winter, water only enough to prevent shriveling. Newly potted plants should not be fertilized the first year; after that, fertilize once every spring with a balanced house-plant fertilizer such as 10-10-10 applied at the strength recommended on the package. For optimum growth, repot annually in the spring, using equal parts of commercial potting soil and sharp sand. Add 1 tablespoon each of ground limestone and bone meal to each gallon of mix. Propagate at any season from stem cuttings or seed.

Outdoors, hardy *O. fragilis* and *O. humifusa* will survive the winter of Zone 4, but should be planted in a sheltered area where they will be shaded from the midday sun. The other opuntias, which are hardy in Zones 9 and 10 from central Texas westward, require full sun. All opuntias need a fast-draining soil. Feed once a year in spring with a balanced fertilizer such as 10-10-10 applied at the strength recommended on the label.

ORANGE COB CACTUS See *Lobivia*
ORGAN-PIPE CACTUS See *Lemaireocereus*
OWL EYES See *Mammillaria*

P

PACHYPHYTUM

P. bracteosum (silver bract); *P. compactum* (thick plant); *P. oviferum* (moonstones, pearly moonstones, sugared almonds) (all called pachyphytum)
Size: 1 to 12 inches tall

Succulent plants native to Mexico, pachyphytums have exceptionally thick, round leaves arranged in rosettes. Bright red bell-shaped flowers blossom in sprays from sides of the plants. Silver bract, growing up to 12 inches tall, has tongue-

TEDDY-BEAR CHOLLA
Opuntia bigelovii

PAPERSPINE CACTUS
Opuntia paediophylla

For climate zones, see map, page 150.

THICK PLANT
Pachyphytum compactum

Parodia erythrantha

shaped light gray leaves that curve upward. This plant's flowers are ½ inch long and blossom in late fall or winter. Thick plant, only 1 to 2 inches tall with ¾- to 1¼-inch-long cylindrical leaves, bears flowers in spring. Moonstones, typically no taller than 2½ inches, has ½- to ¾-inch-long leaves that change from pearly white in winter to pink and mauve under summer sun. All of these pachyphytums do well indoors on a sunny window sill.

HOW TO GROW. Pachyphytums grow best when they receive at least four hours a day of direct sunlight or 12 to 16 hours of strong artificial light. The plants will also grow in bright indirect light. Ideal temperatures range from 50° to 55° at night to 75° or higher during the day. From spring to fall let soil dry moderately between waterings; in winter, water only enough to prevent shriveling. Newly potted plants should not be fed during the first year; after that, fertilize plants once a month during the summer with a standard foliage-house-plant fertilizer such as 10-20-10 diluted to half the strength recommended on the label. When plants become crowded they may be repotted no matter what the season. Plant in equal parts commercial potting soil and sharp sand. Add 1 tablespoon of ground limestone and 1 tablespoon of bone meal to each gallon of mix. Pachyphytums may be propagated at any season from leaf or stem cuttings, or from offsets.

PAINT BRUSH, SCARLET See *Crassula*
PAINTED LADY See *Echeveria*
PALM, NEEDLE See *Yucca*
PALMELLA See *Yucca*
PAPER CACTUS See *Opuntia*
PAPER-SPINE CACTUS See *Opuntia*

PARODIA

P. auriespina (golden Tom Thumb); *P. erythrantha; P. mutabilis* (all called Tom Thumb or parodia)
Size: 2½ to 4 inches tall

Slow-growing but ready to flower after only two or three years, these cacti native to the mountains and open plains of South America are favorites of indoor gardeners. The small globes or cylinders have surfaces of bumps in spirals or straight lines. On the bumps are woolly areoles that bear many spines. From spring through summer, funnel-shaped flowers—often more than three at a time—appear at the top of the plants, and last for five days or longer. Following the flowers come small, dry fruit filled with dustlike seeds. Golden Tom Thumb, its dense network of yellow spines extending up to ¼ inch, resembles a golden ball. Its bright yellow or orange blossoms are generally about 1 inch long. The flowers of *P. erythrantha* are 1¼ inches long. *P. mutabilis,* its red-to-orange central spines protruding ½ inch, bears yellow or orange flowers that may have darker throats.

HOW TO GROW. Four or more hours a day of direct sunlight or strong artificial light for 12 to 16 hours a day are optimum for Tom Thumb cacti. During spring and fall night temperatures of 50° to 60° and day temperatures of 60° to 90° should give way in winter to temperatures of 40° to 50° at night and 70° or less during the day to stimulate flower-bud formation. The soil should become dry to the touch between waterings in spring and fall and be kept moderately moist in summer. In winter, water only enough so that the plants do not shrivel. Forgo feeding newly potted plants for a year; for established plants, each spring apply a high-phosphorus fertilizer such as 15-30-15 at half the strength suggested on the label, or sprinkle a teaspoon of bone meal around each plant. Repotting is only necessary when the plants become over-

136

crowded, and may be done in early spring before flower buds form. Plant in equal parts commercial potting soil and sharp sand. To each gallon of the mixture add 1 tablespoon of ground limestone and 1 tablespoon of bone meal.

PEACOCK ECHEVERIA See *Echeveria*
PEANUT CACTUS See *Chamaecereus*
PEARLY MOONSTONES See *Pachyphytum*
PEBBLES, PRETTY See *Adromischus*

PEDILANTHUS

P. tithymaloides (devil's backbone, redbird cactus, slipper flower)
Size: 3 to 6 feet tall

This subtropical succulent is a distant relative of the familiar Christmas poinsettia. Despite one of its common names, redbird cactus, it is not a cactus and does not have spines. Its fleshy stems contain a poisonous, milky juice that is a skin irritant. The plant does not bear conspicuous flowers; those that sometimes appear from stem tips resemble the heads and wings of birds. With 1- to 3-inch-long leaves, devil's backbone is prized for its zigzagging stems leading from one leaf to the next. It will grow outdoors in hot, humid regions.

HOW TO GROW. Indoors, this succulent grows best in bright but indirect or curtain-filtered sunlight, or under moderate artificial light. High humidity, nighttime temperatures between 50° and 70° and daytime temperatures ranging from 70° to 85° are ideal. Keep the soil barely moist at all times. From early spring to late summer, feed established plants at two- to three-month intervals with a standard house-plant fertilizer such as 5-10-5 used at half the strength recommended on the label. Alternatively, sprinkle a teaspoon of bone meal around each plant each spring. Forgo feeding the rest of the year and never feed newly potted plants during the first six months. Overcrowded plants may be repotted in the spring. Plant in a mixture of equal parts of commercial potting soil and sharp sand. To each gallon of this mix add 1 tablespoon each of bone meal and ground limestone.

Propagate at any season from stem cuttings, letting them dry in the shade for two days before inserting them in sand or a mixture of sand and perlite. Outdoors, devil's backbone is hardy in Zone 10. It thrives in partial shade and well-drained sandy soil. Planting should be done in the spring. Feed every other month from spring to fall with a foliage-house-plant fertilizer such as 5-10-5. Do not feed devil's backbone at all in the winter.

PENCIL LEAF See *Gasteria*

PERESKIA

P. aculeata (lemon vine, leafy cactus, Barbados gooseberry);
P. grandifolia (rose cactus)
Size: Climbing vines up to 30 feet long; shrubs or trees up to 15 feet tall

With their woody stems, roselike flowers and abundant foliage, pereskias are the most primitive and least succulent members of the cactus family. They have sharp, unsheathed spines that grow along their stems and branches; the leaves are usually shed during winter when the plant is dormant. Found in dry tropical regions, pereskias have been used in hedges for centuries by Indians and probably were the first cultivated cacti. Today they are often used as grafting stock for flat-stemmed cacti such as the Christmas cactus. Lemon vine, cultivated by the English as far back as the 17th Century, is a shrubby erect plant when young; with age it becomes a climbing vine that may be over 30 feet long. It

VARIEGATED DEVIL'S BACKBONE
Pedilanthus tithymaloides variegatus

LEMON VINE
Pereskia aculeata

For climate zones, see map, page 150.

MIMICRY PLANT
Pleiospilos bolusii

RAINBOW BUSH
Portulacaria afra variegata

has lemon-scented white, yellow or pink flowers 1 to 1¾ inches across. The blossoms are followed by spiny yellow berries, ¾ inch wide, that are eaten in the West Indies and give the plant one of its common names, Barbados gooseberry. In Brazil, the leaves are cooked as a pot herb.

Rose cactus is a shrublike tree that grows up to 15 feet tall. Its stem is smooth at first, but with age sprouts many 2-inch black spines. The plant bears pink or white flowers, 1½ inches across.

HOW TO GROW. Indoors, pereskias grow best in bright indirect or curtain-filtered sunlight. From spring through fall, night temperatures of 65° to 70° and day temperatures of 75° to 85° are best; in winter, night temperatures of about 50° and day temperatures under 65° will keep the plant from shedding its leaves all at once. Keep the soil moist in summer but dry to the touch between thorough waterings in spring and fall; in winter, water only enough to keep plants from shriveling. Do not fertilize newly potted plants the first year; feed established plants once each year in the spring with a teaspoon of bone meal, or use any house-plant fertilizer at half the strength recommended on the label. Pereskias have rapidly spreading roots and should be repotted early each spring. They may be kept a manageable size indoors by pruning with shears. Plant in a mixture of equal parts of commercial potting soil and sharp sand. Add 1 tablespoon of ground limestone and 1 tablespoon of bone meal to each gallon of mixture. Propagate from cuttings; pereskia cuttings, unlike those of other cacti, should not be dried and callused before rooting.

Outdoors, pereskias are hardy in Zone 10. They grow best in sandy loam and with partial shade. Feed the plants with bone meal once a year in early spring before growth starts. Do not water in winter.

PERUVIAN APPLE CACTUS See *Cereus*
PERUVIAN OLD-MAN CACTUS See *Espostoa*
PHYLLOCACTUS See *Epiphyllum*
PIN WHEEL See *Aeonium*
PINCUSHION, MISSOURI See *Coryphantha*
PINCUSHION, SNOWBALL See *Mammillaria*
PLAID CACTUS See *Gymnocalycium*

PLEIOSPILOS

P. bolusii (mimicry plant, living-rock cactus); *P. nelii* (split rock, cleft stone)
Size: 2 to 3 inches tall

These tiny succulents from southern Africa look more like stones than plants. They have one or two pairs of cradle-shaped leaves with conspicuous spots. In late summer or fall, stemless daisy-like flowers, 2 to 2¾ inches across, appear in the clefts between the leaves. Mimicry plant has brownish-green leaves that are broader than they are long. As many as four golden-yellow flowers may bloom each season on a single plant. Split rock has darker, thicker leaves that are sometimes tinged with red; its 2¾-inch blossoms come in shades of pink, salmon and yellow.

HOW TO GROW. These plants grow best with at least four hours of direct sunlight daily or 12 to 16 hours of strong artificial light. From spring through fall, night temperatures of 50° to 65° and day temperatures between 65° and 80° are best; in winter, provide night temperatures of 40° to 50° and day temperatures under 65°. Let the soil become dry to the touch between thorough waterings from spring through fall; in winter, water only enough to keep plants from shriveling. Do not feed newly potted plants for a year; feed established plants once each spring with a teaspoon of bone meal or with any house-plant fertilizer, such as 5-10-5, diluted to half the strength recommended on the package. Species that form spreading clumps can be repotted in early spring if they become crowded. Use a mixture of 2 parts sharp sand and 1 part commercial potting soil, adding 1 tablespoon each of ground limestone and bone meal to each gallon of mix. Propagate from seeds.

PLOVER EGGS See *Adromischus*
PONY TAIL See *Beaucarnea*

PORTULACARIA
P. afra (elephant bush); *P. afra variegata* (rainbow bush)
Size: Up to 12 feet tall

The elephant bush is a succulent shrub native to arid regions of southern Africa, where it grows in dense thickets. It can reach a height of 12 feet in its natural setting but is often nibbled down by elephants and other animals. The juicy green leaves, ⅓ to ¾ inch long, resemble those of the jade plant; the flowers, tiny and pale pink, rarely bloom on cultivated plants. Rainbow bush, the variegated form, has slightly larger yellow-and-green or pink-and-green leaves.

HOW TO GROW. Indoors, the elephant bush grows best with four hours or more of bright sunlight daily or 12 to 16 hours of bright artificial light. Keep night temperatures between 45° and 55° and day temperatures between 65° and 75° the year round. Allow soil to become dry to the touch between thorough waterings. Do not feed newly potted plants for a year; feed established plants once each spring with a teaspoon of bone meal or with a foliage-house-plant fertilizer applied at the strength recommended on the label. Repot in early spring only when plants become crowded. Pot in a mixture of equal parts of commercial potting soil and sharp sand. Add 1 tablespoon each of ground limestone and bone meal to each gallon of mix. Propagate from cuttings. Elephant bushes can be pruned into bonsai shapes.

Outdoors, the elephant bush is hardy in Zone 10. Plant in full sun or light shade. From spring through fall, feed monthly with a balanced fertilizer such as 10-10-10 at the strength recommended on the label. Do not feed in winter. Let the soil become dry to the touch between thorough waterings.

POSSUM GRAPE See *Cissus*
POWDER-PUFF CACTUS See *Mammillaria*
PRETTY PEBBLES See *Adromischus*
PRIDE, TEXAS See *Thelocactus*
PRISM CACTUS See *Leuchtenbergia*
PROPELLER PLANT See *Crassula*

Q

QUEEN-OF-THE-NIGHT See *Epiphyllum* and *Selenicereus*
QUEEN VICTORIA CENTURY PLANT See *Agave*

R

RAINBOW BUSH See *Portulacaria*
RAINBOW CACTUS See *Echinocereus*
RAINBOW KALANCHOE See *Kalanchoe*
RATTAIL CACTUS See *Aporocactus*
RATTAIL CRASSULA See *Crassula*

REBUTIA
R. krainziana; R. kupperana (scarlet crown cactus); *R. miniscula* (red crown cactus); *R. senilis* (fire crown cactus); *R. violaciflora* (violet crown cactus)
Size: Up to 3 inches tall and 2¾ inches wide

The small size and beautiful, abundant flowers of these

FIRE CROWN CACTUS
Rebutia senilis

For climate zones, see map, page 150.

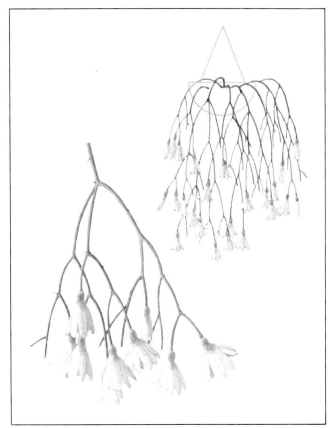

Rhipsalis cribrata

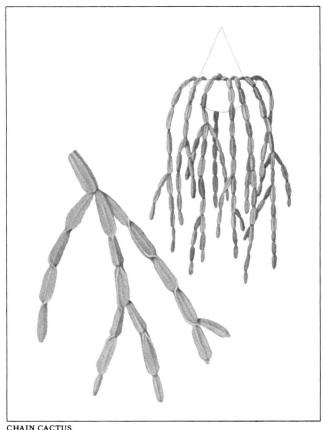

CHAIN CACTUS
Rhipsalis paradoxa

cacti make them popular house plants. Most of them are small bristly globes with dense spiraling lines of projections. At the top of each projection is an areole that sprouts eight to 40 needle-like spines. From spring through summer, masses of funnel-shaped flowers appear on the plants. Each flower lasts four or more days, opening in the morning and closing each night. So great is the array of flowers—a single plant has been known to bear as many as 70 blossoms—that these cacti seem to exhaust themselves in the effort, rarely living more than three or four years. But they produce many offsets to make propagation easy.

R. krainziana looks like a white woolly ball, 2 inches high and 1⅝ inches wide, and bears red flowers up to 1⅝ inches across. Scarlet crown cactus, only 1½ inches wide, is covered with brown needle-like spines, 3/16 inch long; its orange-to-red flowers are 1½ inches long. Red crown cactus bears 1½-inch deep red flowers on 2- to 2½-inch-wide globes covered with white bristle-like spines. Fire crown cactus, 3 inches tall and 2¾ inches thick, is densely covered with white bristle-like spines; its red flowers are 1⅜ inches wide. Violet crown cactus has bristly brown spines about 1 inch long on its flattened 1¼-inch-wide globes; its pink-to-purple flowers are about 1½ inches wide. All of these crown cacti grow well indoors in shallow pots.

HOW TO GROW. Crown cacti grow best with four hours or more of direct sunlight daily, although in the summer they should be shaded from the hot midday sun. If artificial light is used, provide strong light for 12 hours daily. From spring through fall, night temperatures of 50° to 65° and day temperatures of 65° to 85° are best; in winter, provide night temperatures of 40° to 45° and day temperatures under 65°. Let the soil become dry to the touch between thorough waterings while the plant is actively growing. For best blossoms the following year, keep the plant dry after it flowers, watering only enough to keep it from shriveling. When buds start to appear around the base, water lightly and move the cactus to a warmer room. Once the buds turn red, resume regular watering.

Do not fertilize a newly potted plant for a year; feed established plants once each year in the spring with a teaspoon of bone meal or with a standard house-plant fertilizer at half the strength recommended on the label. Repot in early spring in a mixture of equal parts commercial potting soil and sharp sand. Add 1 tablespoon of ground limestone and 1 tablespoon of bone meal to each gallon of mix. Propagate from seed or offsets.

REDBIRD CACTUS See *Pedilanthus*
RED CROWN CACTUS See *Rebutia*
RHIPSALIDOPSIS See *Schlumbergera*

RHIPSALIS
R. cribrata, also called *R. penduliflora; R. paradoxa* (chain cactus, link plant)
Size: Trailing stems up to 3 feet long

With cascading stems and branches that may be cylindrical, flat or angled, these tree-dwelling jungle cacti are suited to display in hanging baskets. Their branches have small areoles with hairs or bristles but usually lack spines; most rhipsalis species have aerial roots. Numerous small flowers up to ¾ inch in size last from one to eight days. Because tiny berry-like fruit follows, rhipsalises are often called mistletoe cacti. *R. cribrata,* while young, has long, thin upright stems that later droop to form whorls of many short branches with only a few bristles and no aerial roots. Its flowers, which are shaped somewhat like bells, are followed by red fruit. Chain cactus looks like a zigzag link chain up to 3 feet long; its branches are about a foot long. Fine hairs or bristles appear on young cacti; older plants have woolly hairs. On established plants, white flowers bloom near the stem tips for as long as three weeks and are followed by small red fruit.

HOW TO GROW. Mistletoe cacti grow best indoors with four hours of bright indirect or curtain-filtered sunlight daily or 10 to 12 hours of moderate artificial light. From spring through fall, provide night temperatures of 50° to 65° and day temperatures of 70° to 85°; in winter, provide night temperatures of 50° to 55° and day temperatures under 65°. Higher winter night temperatures encourage stems to grow rather than flower buds. Maintain relatively high humidity. Pot in a mixture of 2 parts peat moss, 1 part commercial potting soil and 1 part sharp sand or perlite, or use an orchid mixture composed of 2 parts fir bark and 1 part coarse peat moss. Keep the growing medium evenly moist and fertilize every two weeks from spring to late summer with a low-nitrogen house-plant fertilizer such as 5-10-10 diluted according to directions on the label. During the summer, mist plants weekly. For the rest of the year keep the soil drier and do not fertilize the plants. Wait four to six months before feeding newly potted plants. Repot crowded plants in the spring. Propagate from cuttings or by dividing plants.

Mistletoe cacti can be hung outdoors in the shade year round in Zone 10. Elsewhere they can spend the summer under trees but must be brought inside in early autumn.

ROOF HOUSELEEK See *Sempervivum*
ROSARY VINE See *Ceropegia*
ROSEA ICE PLANT See *Mesembryanthemum*
ROSE, DESERT See *Adenium* and *Mesembryanthemum*
ROSE, KAROO See *Lapidaria*
ROSE CACTUS See *Pereskia*
RUBBER PLANT, CHINESE See *Crassula*

S

SAGUARO See *Carnegiea*
SAND DOLLAR See *Astrophytum*

SANSEVIERIA
S. cylindrica (spear sansevieria); *S. trifasciata hahnii* (Hahn's sansevieria, bird's-nest sansevieria)
Size: 6 inches to 5 feet tall

Succulent sansevierias have decorative sword-shaped leaves that rise in circular clusters from thick underground stems. The leaves, fleshy and upright, are marbled in gray, white or green. White or pink flower sprays rarely develop indoors. But sansevierias are among the most dependable of house plants, surviving poor light and extreme dryness. They are also good border plants outdoors in mild climates.

Spear sansevieria, the larger species, has arching dark green leaves up to 5 feet long and 1¼ inches wide that have stripes and crossbands. Hahn's sansevieria, which grows only 6 inches tall, has banded leaves spread out in a 6- to 8-inch rosette resembling a bird's nest or the top of a pineapple.

HOW TO GROW. Sansevierias grow well indoors under a wide variety of light conditions, ranging from nearly full sun to the shadowless light of a north window. Night temperatures of 60° to 70° and day temperatures of 70° to 80° are best year round. From early spring until late fall, let the soil become dry to the touch between thorough waterings; in winter, water just enough to prevent shriveling. Feed established plants every three or four months from early spring until late fall; do not feed the rest of the year. Wait at least four to six months before feeding newly potted plants. Sanse-

HAHN'S SANSEVIERIA
Sansevieria trifasciata hahnii

For climate zones, see map, page 150.

CHRISTMAS CACTUS
Schlumbergera bridgesii

SILVER SQUILL
Scilla violacea

vierias need repotting only every three to five years. When they become crowded, repot at any season in a mixture of 2 parts commercial potting soil to 1 part sharp sand; to a gallon of this mix add 1½ teaspoons of bone meal and 1 tablespoon of ground limestone. Propagate at any season by dividing the underground stems or rooting leaf cuttings in sand.

Outdoors, sansevierias are hardy in Zones 9 and 10. Plants adapt to a sunny spot with some protection from the midday sun or to partial shade; they need a well-drained soil. Plant in the spring. Feed once a year in the spring with a high-phosphorus fertilizer such as 15-30-15 applied at the strength recommended on the label. Do not feed in winter.

SCARLET BALL CACTUS See *Notocactus*
SCARLET BUGLER See *Cleistocactus*
SCARLET CROWN CACTUS See *Rebutia*
SCARLET PAINT BRUSH See *Crassula*

SCHLUMBERGERA
S. bridgesii (Christmas cactus); *S. gaertneri,* also called *Rhipsalidopsis gaertneri* (Easter cactus); *S. truncata,* also called *Zygocactus truncatus* (crab cactus, Thanksgiving cactus)
Size: Trailing stems up to 1½ feet long

These cacti from the rain forests of Brazil are named for their flowering seasons or for the clawlike appearance of their flat stem segments. These segments are up to 2¾ inches long and many of them fork to form multiple chains, long, green and glossy. At their tips in the flowering seasons dangle satiny many-petaled flowers that last several days. Christmas cactus has scalloped stem joints, with rounded tips and one or two indentations along each margin. Between late December and February it bears blossoms about 2½ inches long. The Easter cactus blooms in spring, bearing starlike red flowers 2½ to 3½ inches across at the tips and along the stems where the segments meet. Crab cactus has, along each side of the stem joint, from two to four prominent incurved teeth. Its blossoms are rose-pink, fading back to a whitish bent tube that holds the flower out at an angle from the stem. This plant usually blooms in autumn. Stems of all these cacti grow from 1 to 1½ feet long and are effective tumbling from hanging baskets.

HOW TO GROW. Holiday cacti grow best in bright indirect or curtain-filtered sunlight. Before blooming, they require night temperatures from 50° to 55°. To ensure that Christmas cactus and crab cactus will flower, place plants outdoors from early autumn until just before frost. During this period do not give them any light at night and limit daylight exposure to eight or nine hours daily until buds appear after four or five weeks. Once the buds of any species are set, night temperatures of 60° to 70° and day temperatures of 70° or higher are ideal. Pot in a mixture composed of 2 parts peat moss to 1 part commercial potting soil and 1 part sharp sand or perlite. During the growing season, keep the soil evenly moist and feed once a month with a high-phosphorus fertilizer such as 15-30-15 at the strength recommended on the label. When plants are dormant, water just enough to keep them from shriveling and do not fertilize.

Outdoors these cacti are hardy in Zone 10. Elsewhere they may be kept outdoors in semishade during the summer. Propagate from seeds or from stem cuttings at any time except when the buds are setting.

SCILLA
S. violacea, also called *Ledebouria socialis* (silver squill)
Size: Up to 6 inches tall

Although the silver squill appears to be the same kind of

bulb plant as other more familiar spring-flowering garden squills, it is really a borderline tropical succulent that can only be grown indoors because it is so subject to rot outdoors. From between its mottled-green 2- to 4-inch-long leaves brown flower stems grow 4 to 5 inches tall. In early spring, small bell-shaped flowers appear on four-year-old plants.

HOW TO GROW. Silver squill grows best in bright indirect or curtain-filtered sunlight or 12 hours of artificial light daily. Night temperatures of 50° to 55° and day temperatures of 65° to 85° are best. Pot new bulbs in the early fall in a mixture of 1 part loam, 1 part leaf mold, 1 part sharp sand and ½ part crushed charcoal, or use 2 parts commercial potting soil to 1 part sharp sand. To each gallon of mix add 1 tablespoon of ground limestone and 1 tablespoon of bone meal. Since the silver squill multiplies into large clusters of bulbs with strong roots, use a 10-inch pot to avoid crowding. Store a newly potted plant in a cool, dim place eight to 10 weeks before bringing it into indirect light. Keep the soil moist during active growth. Propagate from offset bulbs.

SEA URCHIN See *Astrophytum*

SEDUM

S. album (white stonecrop); *S. hirsutum; S. lineare variegatum* (carpet sedum); *S. morganianum* (burro's tail, donkey's tail); *S. rubrotinctum* (jelly beans, Christmas cheer); *S. sieboldi* (October plant, October daphne); *S. spathulifolium; S. spectabile* (showy stonecrop, live-forever); *S. weinbergii,* also called *Graptopetalum paraguayense* (ghost plant, mother-of-pearl) (all called sedum)
Size: 3 inches to 2 feet tall; trailing stems up to 3 feet long

The popular, adaptable sedums are low-growing succulents with creeping stems, often no more than 3 or 4 inches tall. They have small, fleshy evergreen or semievergreen leaves in a variety of sizes, shapes and colors. Their starlike flowers bloom at intervals throughout the year depending on the species and the location. White stonecrop, a ground cover, has stems 2 to 3 inches tall bearing ¼-inch evergreen leaves with tips tinged red in winter. In late summer it produces ¼-inch white flowers. *S. hirsutum* has spicy-smelling leaves, ⅜ inch long, in crowded rosettes. The ½-inch-wide white flowers, often veined with red, bloom from late winter to summer. Carpet sedum grows 6 inches tall or more; its pointed leaves, ¾ to 1¼ inches long, are edged with white. Yellow flowers ⅝ inch wide bloom in the late spring or early summer. Trailing burro's tail has flimsily attached inch-long tear-shaped leaves that overlap so closely the stems resemble long braids; 1 to 1½ inches thick, they are 1½ to 3 feet long. The yellow-green leaves are covered with a powdery-blue dustlike bloom. In spring, burro's tail produces ½-inch deep-rose-colored flowers.

Jelly beans, which is one of the most vigorous of the sedums, has fat ½- to ¾-inch green leaves with reddish-brown tips; in the bright sun the leaf tips turn red. The plants bear clusters of yellow flowers in winter or spring. October plant has purplish stems that usually grow 6 to 9 inches long and are covered with whorls of three round, ½-inch leaves with wavy edges. In the fall, rounded clusters of ½-inch-wide pink flowers appear at the tips, then plants die down to the ground in winter. *S. spathulifolium* has rosettes of leaves ½ to 1¼ inches long growing on top of forking branches. Its ⅝-inch yellow flowers bloom in the late spring. Showy stonecrop has soft, toothed leaves up to 3 inches long and 2 inches wide arranged in twos, threes or fours along 12- to 22-inch stems. In late summer, clusters of flowers in various shades of rose bloom. Ghost plant gets its name from

CARPET SEDUM
Sedum lineare variegatum

JELLY BEANS
Sedum rubrotinctum

For climate zones, see map, page 150.

SHOWY STONECROP
Sedum spectabile

GHOST PLANT
Sedum weinbergii

the bluish sheen of the ½- to 1-inch-wide leaves that grow in rosettes on trailing stems up to 1 foot long. The ¾-inch green-and-white flowers bloom in the late winter or early spring. Sedums are suitable plants for rock gardens and flower borders; those with trailing stems will cascade from hanging baskets.

HOW TO GROW. Sedums grow well indoors where they get four hours or more a day of direct sunlight, or from 12 to 16 hours of strong artificial light; they grow fairly well in bright indirect light. In spring, summer and fall, night temperatures of 50° to 65° and day temperatures of 68° to 90° are suitable. In winter, give them night temperatures of 40° to 50° and day temperatures up to 65°. Let the soil become dry to the touch between thorough waterings; for plants that become semidormant during the winter, such as showy stonecrop and October plant, water only enough to keep the leaves from shriveling during this period.

Feed established plants three times a year—in very early spring, late spring and late summer, using a house-plant fertilizer such as 10-20-10 at half the strength recommended on the label. Do not feed plants the rest of the year, and wait four to six months before feeding newly potted plants. Trailing plants rarely need repotting. Because the stems of burro's tail are so brittle, it is better to feed and water old, crowded plants more often than attempt to repot them. When repotting of any sedum is necessary, use a mixture of 1 part commercial potting soil and 1 part sharp sand. Add 1 tablespoon of ground limestone and 1 tablespoon of bone meal to each gallon of mix. Propagate in any season from cuttings or by dividing plants.

Outdoors, white stonecrop, October plant, *S. spathulifolium* and showy stonecrop can be grown in Zones 3-10 except on the Gulf Coast. Most other sedums grow well outdoors in Zones 9 and 10. All need full sun or light shade. Most tolerate almost any well-drained soil, adapting to poor soil and dry locations; exceptions are *S. spathulifolium,* which does better in light, moist humus, and burro's tail, which needs protection from wind and rain. Plant at any time when the soil can be prepared, placing plants 9 to 12 inches apart. Do not fertilize.

SELENICEREUS

S. grandiflorus (queen-of-the-night, night-blooming cereus)
Size: Up to 16 feet long

A West Indian cactus, queen-of-the-night fills the evening air with the vanilla-like scent of its giant blossoms, then closes at the approach of dawn. This tree-dwelling cactus has long five- to eight-ribbed stems that can grow up to 16 feet long and 1 inch thick, producing short, sharp spines and many climbing air roots. The stems, which grow as much as a yard each year, can be trained to climb an indoor trellis or an outdoor post or tree. Immense white flowers, 7 to 10 inches long, grow only on long-established plants.

HOW TO GROW. Queen-of-the-night grows best in bright indirect or curtain-filtered sunlight and relatively high humidity. From spring through fall, keep night temperatures between 60° and 65° and day temperatures between 70° and 85°; in winter provide night temperatures of 50° to 55° and day temperatures under 65°. (Higher night temperatures in winter prevent the formation of flower buds.) Pot in a mixture of 2 parts peat moss, 1 part commercial potting soil and 1 part sharp sand or perlite; or use an orchid mixture composed of 1 part fir bark and 1 part coarse peat moss. Keep the growing medium evenly moist and fertilize every two weeks from spring to late summer with a low-nitrogen house-plant fertilizer such as 5-10-10 diluted to half the strength recommended on the label; during the summer, mist plants each week. For the rest of the year keep plants fairly dry and do not fertilize them. Wait four to six months before feeding newly potted plants. Outdoors it can be grown in well-drained soil in Zone 10 and Zone 9 in the Southwest. Propagate from tip or joint cuttings at any time.

SEMPERVIVUM
S. arachnoideum (cobweb houseleek, spiderweb houseleek); *S. tectorum* (common houseleek, roof houseleek, hen-and-chickens, old-man-and-woman)
Size: ½ to 4 inches wide

Houseleeks are succulent alpine perennials with fleshy, wedge-shaped leaves growing in small rosettes. Miniatures of the mature plant surround the main rosettes like chicks around a mother hen. In summer, mature plants send up flower stalks. The red flowers of the cobweb houseleek are borne on 3- to 5-inch flower stalks, while the common houseleek has stalks up to 18 inches tall bearing purplish-red flowers. After blooming, the main rosette usually dies, but the small ones continue to grow and spread as a colony.

Cobweb houseleek has rosettes that may be less than an inch across. Their leaves are connected by strands of fine cobweb-like white hairs; the outermost leaves are usually tinged brown-red. Common houseleeks, once grown on the thatched rooftops of Eastern Europe, have rosettes 3 to 4 inches wide with bristly tips. Both low-growing plants are suitable for rock gardens, wall crevices or flower borders and grow well indoors on a sunny window sill.

HOW TO GROW. Indoors, houseleeks grow best where they get four hours or more of direct sunlight daily, or from 12 to 16 hours of strong artificial light. Cobweb houseleek needs winter night temperatures of 40° to 45° and day temperatures of 55° to 60°. In summer it grows best with night temperatures of 60° to 65° and day temperatures of 75° to 80°. For the common houseleek, winter night temperatures of 50° to 55° and day temperatures of 60° to 72° are best. In summer, it needs night temperatures of 70° to 75° and day temperatures of 80° to 90°. From spring to fall, let the soil become dry to the touch between thorough waterings; in winter, water only enough to keep the plants from shriveling. Do not fertilize newly potted plants for a year; feed established plants once each spring, sprinkling a teaspoon of bone meal around the base of each plant. Or use any house-plant fertilizer such as 5-10-5 applied at half the strength recommended on the label. Repot in early spring in a mixture of equal parts of commercial soil and sharp sand. Add 1 tablespoon of ground limestone and 1 tablespoon of bone meal to each gallon of mix. Propagate from offsets at any season.

Outdoors, houseleeks are hardy in Zones 3-10 except on the Gulf Coast. They grow well in full sun or light shade and will tolerate almost any well-drained soil. Plant offsets at any time of the year when the soil can be prepared, spacing plants 6 to 9 inches apart. New offsets will rapidly fill the open spaces. Do not fertilize.

SEMPERVIVUM See also *Aichryson* and *Greenovia*
SENITA See *Lophocereus*
SHORT-LEAVED ALOE See *Aloe*
SHOWY STONECROP See *Sedum*
SILVER BALL CACTUS See *Notocactus*
SILVER BRACT See *Pachyphytum*
SILVER CROWN See *Cotyledon*
SILVER DOLLAR PLANT See *Crassula*
SILVER TORCH See *Cleistocactus*
SLIPPER FLOWER See *Pedilanthus*

For climate zones, see map, page 150.

QUEEN-OF-THE-NIGHT
Selenicereus grandiflorus

COBWEB HOUSELEEK
Sempervivum arachnoideum

NOBLE STAR FLOWER
Stapelia nobilis

GLORY-OF-TEXAS
Thelocactus bicolor

SNOWBALL, MEXICAN See *Echeveria*
SNOWBALL CACTUS See *Espostoa*
SNOWBALL PINCUSHION See *Mammillaria*
SOAP TREE See *Yucca*
SOAPWEED See *Yucca*
SPIDER ALOE See Aloe
SPIDER CACTUS See *Gymnocalycium*
SPIDERWEB HOUSELEEK See *Sempervivum*
SPLIT ROCK See *Pleiospilos*
SQUILL, SILVER See *Scilla*

STAPELIA
S. gigantea (giant toad plant, Zulu giant); *S. nobilis* (noble star flower) (both called carrion flower, toad flower)
Size: Up to 1 foot tall

Notable for their gigantic blossoms, carrion flowers are magnificent plants, though best admired at a distance when in flower because of their unpleasant smell. These succulents form clumps of fleshy, leafless stems that are usually four-sided. In spring, they bear puffy, starlike flowers, up to 16 inches wide, that attract flies. The stems of the giant toad plant can grow 10 to 12 inches tall; its enormous yellow flower, ridged with red and downy with fine purplish hairs, is 10 to 16 inches wide. Noble star flower has branching stems up to 8 inches long, their edges lined with tiny teeth. Plants bear 1-foot-wide blossoms covered with fine hairs.

HOW TO GROW. Indoors, carrion flowers grow best with four hours or more of bright indirect sunlight a day. They grow fairly well with 12 to 16 hours a day of strong artificial light. From spring to fall, night temperatures of 50° to 65° and day temperatures of 65° to 85° are best; in winter, night temperatures of 45° to 50° and day temperatures under 65° are ideal. Keep the soil moist but not soggy during the growing season. After they flower, water the plants only enough to keep them from shriveling. Pot in a mixture of 1 part commercial potting soil and 1 part sharp sand, with 1 tablespoon of ground limestone and 1 tablespoon of bone meal added to each gallon of mix. Cut back the stems each fall or start new plants from cuttings, since flowers develop only on new growth. When they blossom, set plants outside to avoid the odor. Propagate from cuttings or seeds or by dividing plants.

STAR CACTUS See *Ariocarpus* and *Astrophytum*
STAR FLOWER, NOBLE See *Stapelia*
STRAWBERRY HEDGEHOG See *Echinocereus*
STRING-OF-BEADS See *Kleinia*
STRING-OF-BUTTONS See *Crassula*
SUGARED ALMONDS See *Pachyphytum*
SUN CUP See *Notocactus*

T

TAIL, BURRO'S See *Sedum*
TAIL, DONKEY'S See *Sedum*
TEDDY-BEAR CHOLLA See *Opuntia*
TEXAS PRIDE See *Thelocactus*
THANKSGIVING CACTUS See *Schlumbergera*

THELOCACTUS
T. bicolor (glory-of-Texas, Texas pride); *T. nidulans* (bird's-nest cactus)
Size: Up to 8 inches tall

One of the most decorative cacti of the deserts of Mexico and southern Texas, thelocacti have grooved ribs, formed by protuberances which sprout multicolored spines. They usually grow in clusters of round or cone-shaped stems, 3 to 8 inches tall and 2 to 8 inches wide. On older plants, showy flowers, which open on summer days to a width of as much as 2½ inches, are followed by scaly fruit. Glory-of-Texas sometimes forms cones 8 inches tall and 3 inches thick. Red or yellow-and-red spines grow on the ribs of the plant; flower colors range from pink to violet. Bird's-nest cactus does not form clusters but remains a solitary flattened globe 4 inches tall and 8 inches wide with a prickly mat of wool and fiber that resembles a nest on top. Young plants have 13 to 15 brown spines per areole, while older ones have four to six. Flowers are pale yellow. Both thelocactus species can be grown indoors in pots or outdoors where the climate permits in borders and rock gardens.

HOW TO GROW. Thelocacti grow well indoors with four hours or more of direct sunlight or 12 to 16 hours of bright artificial light daily; they do fairly well in bright indirect light. From spring through fall, night temperatures of 50° to 55° and day temperatures between 65° and 70° suit them best; in winter, provide night temperatures of 40° to 45° and day temperatures under 65°. Let the soil become dry to the touch between thorough waterings from spring through fall; in winter, water only enough to keep plants from shriveling. Do not feed newly potted plants for a year; feed established plants once each spring, sprinkling a teaspoon of bone meal around the base of each plant, or use any house-plant fertilizer at half the strength recommended on the label. Plants grow slowly and need repotting only every three to five years. Plant in a mixture of 2 parts commercial potting soil to 1 part sharp sand; add 1 tablespoon of ground limestone and 1 tablespoon of bone meal to each gallon of this mixture. Propagate from cuttings.

Outdoors, thelocacti grow well in Zones 9 and 10, thriving in full sun and well-drained soil. Plant in the spring. From spring to fall, feed monthly with a phosphorus-rich fertilizer such as 15-30-15, applied at the strength recommended on the label. Do not feed in the winter.

THICK PLANT See *Pachyphytum*
THORNS, CROWN-OF- See *Euphorbia*
THREAD-BEARING CENTURY PLANT See *Agave*
TIGER ALOE See *Aloe*
TIGER JAWS See *Faucaria*
TOAD PLANT, GIANT See *Stapelia*
TOES, BABY See *Mesembryanthemum*
TOES, BEAR'S See *Cotyledon*
TOM-THUMB See *Parodia*
TOTEM-POLE CACTUS See *Lophocereus*
TRAILING ICE PLANT See *Mesembryanthemum*
TREE, BLACK See *Aeonium*
TREE, ELEPHANT See *Bursera*
TREE, ELEPHANT-FOOT See *Beaucarnea*
TREE, JOSHUA See *Yucca*
TREE, SOAP See *Yucca*

TRICHOCEREUS
T. shaferi
Size: Up to 20 inches tall

Young plants of this South American mountain cactus are covered with white down and have yellow-green stems, but on older plants the stems are dark green and covered with yellowish needle-like spines ½ inch long. After the plants are five years old, they produce fragrant funnel-shaped flowers 6 to 7 inches long that bloom during summer nights. Trichocereus plants, because they grow up to 20 inches tall and 4 or 5 inches thick, are often used as stock for grafting other cacti.

HOW TO GROW. *T. shaferi* grows best indoors with four

Trichocereus shaferi

For climate zones, see map, page 150.

hours or more of direct sunlight daily or from 12 to 16 hours of strong light; it will grow fairly well in bright indirect light. From spring through fall, night temperatures of 50° to 60° and day temperatures between 65° and 90° are best; in winter, provide night temperatures of 40° to 45° and day temperatures under 65°. Let the soil become moderately dry between thorough waterings from spring through fall; in winter, water only enough to keep the plants from shriveling. Do not fertilize newly potted plants for a year; feed established plants once each spring, sprinkling a teaspoon of bone meal around the base of each plant, or use house-plant fertilizer such as 5-10-5 at half the strength recommended on the label. Repot in early spring only when plants become crowded. Use a mixture of equal parts commercial potting soil and sharp sand, adding 1 tablespoon of ground limestone and 1 tablespoon of bone meal to each gallon of mix. Propagate from cuttings or seeds.

Outdoors, *T. shaferi* is hardy in Zone 10 and in Zone 9 in Arizona and Southern California. Plants grow best in full sun. They will tolerate poor soil if it is well drained. Plant in the spring. Each spring feed with a sprinkling of bone meal.

TRICHODIADEMA See *Mesembryanthemum*
TRUE ALOE See *Aloe*
TURK'S CAP, DWARF See *Melocactus*

V

VARIEGATED CENTURY PLANT See *Agave*
VELDT IVY See *Cissus*
VELVET LEAF See *Kalanchoe*
VINE, HEART See *Ceropegia*
VINE, LEMON See *Pereskia*
VINE, NECKLACE See *Crassula*
VINE, ROSARY See *Ceropegia*
VIOLET CROWN CACTUS See *Rebutia*
VISNAGA See *Ferocactus*

W

WART PLANT See *Haworthia*
WASHBOARD, FAIRY See *Haworthia*
WAX AGAVE See *Echeveria*
WHEEL, PIN See *Aeonium*
WHISKER CACTUS See *Lophocereus*
WHITE STONECROP See *Sedum*
WHITE-WEB BALL CACTUS See *Notocactus*

WILCOXIA

W. schmollii, also called *W. senilis* (lamb's-tail cactus)
Size: Trailing stems 10 inches long

The lamb's-tail cactus has weak, slender stems that grow pendant from protruding tuberous roots. Its inconspicuous ribs are covered with clusters of soft bristles. The flowers, up to 1¼ inches long, last several days and bloom on young as well as mature plants, opening in late afternoon.

The lamb's-tail cactus, native to central Mexico, has green stems 10 inches long and ⅝ inch thick produced from a tuber up to 3 inches thick. As the plant ages the stems yellow near the base. The nine to 10 low ribs are covered with white hairlike spines. Pale rose-purple flowers, 1¼ inches long, are followed by spiny fruits. Wilcoxias are frequently grafted onto other types of cacti.

HOW TO GROW. Indoors, the lamb's-tail cactus grows best in direct sunlight. During the winter, night temperatures of 40° to 45° and day temperatures under 65° are ideal. From spring through autumn, night temperatures of 65° to 70° and day temperatures between 75° and 80° are recommended.

LAMB'S-TAIL CACTUS
Wilcoxia schmollii

From spring through autumn, allow the top soil in the container to become dry to the touch, then water thoroughly. During the winter, water just enough to keep stems from withering. Newly potted plants should not be fertilized in the first year. Fertilize established plants biweekly through spring and summer with a high-phosphorus fertilizer such as 15-30-15, diluted to half the strength recommended on the label. Plant the lamb's-tail cactus in a container large enough to accommodate the tuberous root system, or growth may be stunted. As soon as a plant becomes crowded, repot it in equal parts of commercial potting soil and sharp sand. Add 1 tablespoon of limestone and 1 tablespoon of bone meal for each gallon of mix. Propagate at any season from stem-tip cuttings rooted in moist vermiculite, or from seed.

WINDOW PLANT See *Haworthia*

Y

YOUTH-AND-OLD-AGE See *Aichryson*

YUCCA

Y. brevifolia (Joshua tree); *Y. elata* (soap tree, soapweed, palmella); *Y. filamentosa* (Adam's needle, needle palm)
Size: 2½ to 20 feet tall; leaves up to 3 feet long

Yuccas are often called the giant lilies of North America; they are semisucculent dry-climate plants frequently used in cactus and succulent gardens. Some are stemless; others are treelike with erect woody stems that are often branched. All have evergreen rosettes of stiff, sword-shaped, often fibrous leaves. They produce enormous clusters of cup-shaped flowers, usually creamy white, on tall stalks from the center of the rosette. The flowers resemble giant lilies of the valley; some people find their scent unpleasant.

The Joshua tree is native to the high deserts of California, Nevada, Utah and Arizona. Named by Mormon pioneers for the Biblical patriarch, this plant on rare occasions reaches a monumental 40 feet in height. It has a palmlike stem that grows up to 3 feet thick. The plant usually branches, producing irregular stems that bear leaves 14 inches long and ⅝ inch wide with tiny teeth along their edges. Small waxy green-white flowers grow in clusters more than a foot long. Joshua tree blooms from February to April. The soap tree has stems that are up to 15 feet tall and bears white flower clusters up to 7 feet long. Pale green leaves 38 inches long and 1 inch wide have margins that are paler in color and bear fine, threadlike strands.

Adam's needle is nearly stemless with showy, drooping spine-tipped leaves 2½ feet long and 1 inch wide. The leaf margins bear curly white hairs. Summer flowers, each 2 inches long, grow in 3- to 6-foot sprays. This species is hardy even where frost is severe and is a bold landscape accent.

HOW TO GROW. Outdoors, the Joshua tree is hardy in Zones 7-10, Adam's needle in Zones 4-10, the soap tree in Zones 9 and 10 and in Zone 8 from central Texas westward. The yuccas need good drainage and light, sandy, dry soil. They grow best in full or partial sun. Fertilize once a year by working a handful of bone meal into the soil around each plant. Propagate at any season from small plantlets that appear at the bases of established plants. Spring and fall are the best seasons for propagating by root division or by seed. Yuccas are rarely grown indoors as house plants.

Yucca filamentosa 'Bright Edge'

Z

ZEBRA HAWORTHIA See *Haworthia*
ZULU GIANT See *Stapelia*
ZYGOCACTUS See *Schlumbergera*

For climate zones, see map, page 150.

Where cacti and succulents survive outdoors

Most cacti and other succulents can be grown in year-round outdoor gardens only in regions that are frost-free. But some of these plants, such as certain species of *Opuntia, Sedum* and *Sempervivum,* will survive winters where the temperature drops well below freezing.

The map below, based on official weather records, divides North America into several numbered zones based on the range of winter temperatures. Plants described in the encyclopedia that can be grown outdoors are given zone numbers corresponding with this map to help you determine which plants can be grown successfully in your area of the country.

Experimentation may pay off. Some plants can survive somewhat colder climates than indicated if they are planted in a sheltered location in fast-draining soil. Others will survive in certain parts of a zone; *Lemaireocereus* species, for example, thrive in the dry western reaches of Zone 8, but not in its high-humidity regions to the east.

Some plants have peculiar growth cycles owing to their places of origin. Many of the plants that are natives of the Southern Hemisphere, such as species of *Bowiea* and *Schlumbergera,* have not adjusted to the reverse growing season of the Northern Hemisphere and are unsuitable for outdoor planting in North America. But others of their ilk, such as certain species of *Chamaecereus* and *Haworthia,* make the change quite readily.

If you decide to move your indoor plants out to the terrace for the months of summer, condition them gradually to bright sunlight. They are otherwise susceptible to severe sunburn.

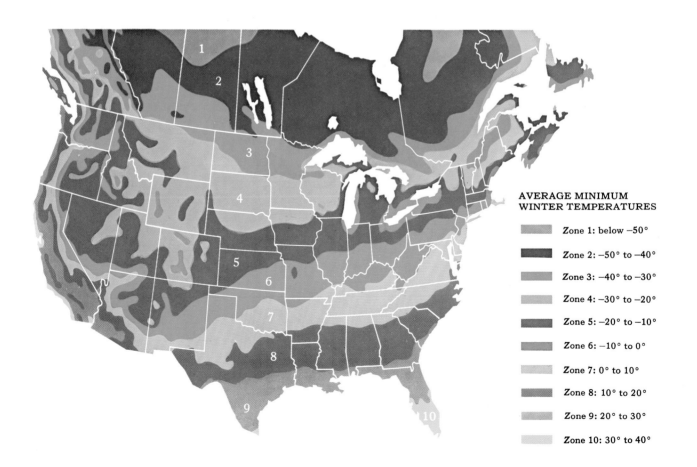

AVERAGE MINIMUM WINTER TEMPERATURES

Zone 1: below −50°
Zone 2: −50° to −40°
Zone 3: −40° to −30°
Zone 4: −30° to −20°
Zone 5: −20° to −10°
Zone 6: −10° to 0°
Zone 7: 0° to 10°
Zone 8: 10° to 20°
Zone 9: 20° to 30°
Zone 10: 30° to 40°

Characteristics of 108 cacti and succulents

Listed below for quick reference are the species illustrated in Chapter 5.

	PLANT HEIGHT*			FLOWER COLOR					BLOOMING SEASONS				SPECIAL USES						LIGHT			NIGHT TEMP.		
	Under 1 foot	1 to 2 feet	Over 2 feet	White-green	Yellow-orange	Pink-red	Blue-purple	Multicolor	Winter	Spring	Summer	Fall	Potted plant	Dish garden	Hanging basket	Rock garden	Ground cover	Specimen plant	Bright direct	Indirect or filtered	Artificial	45° to 55°	50° to 60°	60° to 70°
ADENIUM OBESUM (desert rose)			●			●					●		●					●	●	●	●		●	
ADROMISCHUS FESTIVUS (plover eggs)		●		●	●						●		●	●		●		●	●	●			●	
AEONIUM ARBOREUM ATROPURPUREUM (black tree)			●		●		●				●		●	●	●	●		●	●	●			●	
AEONIUM HAWORTHII (pin wheel)		●		●	●					●			●	●	●	●		●	●	●			●	
AGAVE AMERICANA MARGINATA (variegated century plant)		●	●	●							●		●					●	●	●	●			
AGAVE UNIVITTATA		●		●							●		●	●				●	●	●	●			
AICHRYSON DICHOTOMUM	●				●					●			●	●		●			●	●		●		
ALLUAUDIA HUMBERTII		●									●		●	●		●		●	●	●				
ALOE HUMILIS (crocodile jaws)	●				●		●				●		●	●		●		●	●	●				
ANACAMPSEROS ALSTONII	●			●		●					●		●	●					●	●				
APOROCACTUS FLAGELLIFORMIS (rattail cactus)		●	●			●				●			●		●			●	●	●		●		
ARIOCARPUS FISSURATUS (star cactus)	●			●	●				●	●	●	●	●	●		●		●	●	●		●		
ASTROPHYTUM ASTERIAS (sand dollar)	●				●						●		●	●				●	●	●				
ASTROPHYTUM MYRIOSTIGMA (bishop's cap)	●				●						●		●	●				●	●	●				
BEAUCARNEA RECURVATA (pony tail)		●	●										●					●	●	●				
BOWIEA VOLUBILIS (climbing onion)		●	●			●						●			●			●	●	●		●		
BURSERA MICROPHYLLA (elephant tree)		●		●							●		●	●				●	●	●	●			●
CARALLUMA EUROPAEA	●					●	●				●		●	●		●			●	●		●		
CARNEGIEA GIGANTEA (saguaro)	●	●	●							●	●		●	●		●		●	●	●				
CEPHALOCEREUS CHRYSACANTHUS (golden old-man cactus)	●				●						●		●	●		●		●	●	●				
CEREUS PERUVIANUS (Peruvian apple cactus)		●	●	●		●					●		●	●		●		●	●	●				
CEROPEGIA WOODII (rosary vine)		●	●			●						●			●				●	●		●		
CHAMAECEREUS SILVESTRII (peanut cactus)	●				●	●				●			●					●	●	●				
CISSUS QUADRANGULARIS (Veldt ivy)		●	●	●							●		●		●			●		●				
CLEISTOCACTUS STRAUSII (silver torch)		●			●	●				●	●		●					●	●	●	●			
CONOPHYTUM MINUTUM	●				●		●			●	●		●	●					●		●	●	●	
CONOPHYTUM SPRINGBOKENSE	●				●		●			●	●		●	●					●		●	●	●	
CORYPHANTHA CLAVA	●			●							●		●	●		●		●		●				
COTYLEDON UNDULATA (silver crown)	●			●	●						●		●				●	●						●
CRASSULA ARBORESCENS (silver dollar plant)		●	●	●		●					●		●	●				●	●	●	●			
CRASSULA PERFORATA (necklace vine)		●		●							●		●	●				●	●	●				
ECHEVERIA AGAVOIDES (wax agave)	●					●			●	●			●	●		●		●	●	●			●	●
ECHEVERIA HYBRID 'BALLERINA'	●					●			●	●			●	●		●		●	●	●			●	●
ECHINOCACTUS INGENS (large barrel cactus)		●		●							●		●			●	●	●		●				
ECHINOCEREUS ENGELMANNII (strawberry hedgehog)	●					●				●			●					●		●				
ECHINOCEREUS PECTINATUS (rainbow cactus)	●				●						●		●					●		●				
ECHINOFOSSULOCACTUS MULTICOSTATUS (brain cactus)	●		●								●		●			●		●		●				
ECHINOPSIS HYBRID 'HAKU JO'	●		●	●							●		●					●	●	●				
ECHINOPSIS LONGISPINA	●		●								●		●					●	●	●				
EPIPHYLLUM HYBRID 'PAUL DE LONGPRE'		●	●		●			●	●	●	●	●	●		●			●	●	●				
EPITHELANTHA MICROMERIS (button cactus)	●			●						●			●	●		●		●		●				
ESPOSTOA LANATA (Peruvian old-man cactus)	●	●	●								●		●					●	●	●				
EUPHORBIA GRANDICORNIS (cow's horn)		●		●							●		●			●	●	●	●	●				
EUPHORBIA OBESA (basketball euphorbia)	●		●								●		●	●				●		●				
FAUCARIA TIGRINA (tiger jaws)	●				●							●	●	●				●		●				
FEROCACTUS ACANTHODES (fishhook)	●	●	●								●		●					●		●		●		
FOUQUIERA FASCICULATA		●	●	●						●	●		●					●	●		●		●	●
GASTERIA LILIPUTANA	●		●								●		●	●				●	●	●				
GREENOVIA AUREA	●			●							●		●	●					●				●	●
GYMNOCALYCIUM GRAFT (moon cactus)	●						●			●	●		●	●				●		●				

In the case of trailing plants, figures given apply to length of stems.

	Under 1 foot	1 to 2 feet	Over 2 feet	White-green	Yellow-orange	Pink-red	Blue-purple	Multicolor	Winter	Spring	Summer	Fall	Potted plant	Dish garden	Hanging basket	Rock garden	Ground cover	Specimen plant	Bright direct	Indirect or filtered	Artificial	45° to 55°	50° to 60°	60° to 70°
	PLANT HEIGHT*			**FLOWER COLOR**					**BLOOMING SEASONS**				**SPECIAL USES**						**LIGHT**			**NIGHT TEMP.**		
GYMNOCALYCIUM QUEHLIANUM	•		•		•				•	•			•	•					•			•		
HARRISIA MARTINII	•		•						•	•			•	•	•				•	•		•		
HATIORA SALICORNIOIDES (dancing bones)	•	•			•	•		•					•		•				•			•		
HAWORTHIA LIMIFOLIA (fairy washboard)	•												•	•					•	•		•		
HUERNIA MACROCARPA	•			•		•			•	•	•	•	•					•	•	•		•		
KALANCHOE BEHARENSIS (velvet leaf)		•		•		•							•				•	•				•		
KALANCHOE FEDTSCHENKOI (rainbow kalanchoe)		•		•		•							•		•			•				•		
KLEINIA ROWLEYANUS (string-of-beads)		•	•						•	•	•	•			•			•	•	•		•		
KLEINIA STAPELIIFORMIS	•				•							•	•					•	•	•		•		
LAPIDARIA MARGARETAE (Karoo rose)	•				•						•	•	•	•				•	•				•	•
LEMAIREOCEREUS THURBERI (organ-pipe cactus)		•	•			•					•		•				•	•	•	•		•		
LEUCHTENBERGIA PRINCIPIS (agave cactus)	•				•								•					•					•	•
LITHOPS BROMFIELDII (living stones)	•			•	•						•	•	•					•				•	•	•
LITHOPS DIVERGENS (living stones)	•				•						•	•	•					•					•	•
LITHOPS FULVICEPS LACTINEA (living stones)	•			•	•						•	•	•					•					•	•
LITHOPS OLIVACEA (living stones)	•				•						•	•	•					•					•	•
LITHOPS OPTICA RUBRA (living stones)	•				•						•	•	•					•					•	•
LITHOPS SALICOLA (living stones)	•			•							•	•	•					•					•	•
LITHOPS TURBINIFORMIS (living stones)	•			•							•	•	•					•				•		
LOBIVIA HERTRICHIANA	•	•				•				•	•	•	•					•	•	•		•		
LOPHOCEREUS SCHOTTII MONSTROSUS (totem-pole cactus)		•				•			•	•			•				•	•	•			•		
MAMMILLARIA CAMPTOTRICHA (bird's-nest cactus)	•		•						•	•			•	•				•				•	•	
MAMMILLARIA HAHNIANA (old-lady cactus)	•					•	•			•			•	•				•				•	•	
MAMMILLARIA PARKINSONII (owl eyes)	•			•						•			•	•				•				•	•	
MAMMILLARIA PLUMOSA (feather cactus)	•			•				•					•	•				•				•	•	
MELOCACTUS MATANZANUS (dwarf Turk's cap)	•				•			•					•	•				•	•	•		•		
MESEMBRYANTHEMUM EDULE (Hottentot fig)	•				•	•	•			•			•			•	•	•	•			•		
MESEMBRYANTHEMUM RHOPALOPHYLLUM (baby toes)	•				•					•	•		•	•				•		•		•		
MYRTILLOCACTUS GEOMETRIZANS (blue flame)		•	•										•				•	•					•	•

*In the case of trailing plants, figures given apply to length of stems.

Bibliography

Alexander, E. J., *Succulent Plants of New and Old World Deserts.* New York Botanical Garden, 1950.

Bailey, Ralph, *The Good Housekeeping Illustrated Encyclopedia of Gardening.* Hearst Magazines, 1971.

Benson, Lyman, *The Cacti of Arizona,* 3rd ed. The University of Arizona Press, 1969.

Benson, Lyman, *The Native Cacti of California.* Stanford University Press, 1969.

Britton, Nathaniel L., and Rose, J. N., *The Cactaceae: Descriptions and Illustrations of Plants of the Cactus Family.* Dover Publications, Inc., 1963.

Brooklyn Botanic Garden, *Handbook on Miniature Gardens.* BBG, 1968.

Brooklyn Botanic Garden, *Handbook on Succulent Plants.* BBG, 1963.

Castle, Lewis, *Cactaceous Plants: Their History and Culture.* The Runeskald Press, 1974.

Chidamian, Claude, *Cacti and Other Succulents.* The American Garden Guild and Doubleday & Co., Inc., 1958.

Chittenden, Fred J., ed., *The Royal Horticultural Society Dictionary of Gardening,* 2nd ed. Clarendon Press, 1974.

Consumer Guide Editors, *Cacti and Other Succulents.* Consumer Guide, 1976.

Cutak, Ladislaus, *Cactus Guide.* D. Van Nostrand Co., Inc., 1956.

Davidson, William, and Rochford, T. C., *The Complete All-Color Guide to House Plants: Cacti and Succulents.* The Hamlyn Publishing Group, Ltd., London, 1976.

Everett, T. H., *New Illustrated Encyclopedia of Gardening.* Greystone Press, 1960.

Foster, H. Lincoln, *Rock Gardening.* Houghton Mifflin Co., 1968.

Glass, Charles, and Foster, Robert, *Cacti and Succulents for the Amateur.* Van Nostrand Reinhold Co., 1976.

Graf, Alfred Byrd, *Exotic Plant Manual: Exotic Plants to Live With.* Roehrs Co., Inc., 1974.

Graf, Alfred Byrd, *Exotica: Pictorial Cyclopedia of Exotic Plants from Tropical and Near-topic Regions.* Roehrs Co., Inc., 1973.

Herwig, Rob, and Schubert, Margot, *The Treasury of House-

	PLANT HEIGHT*			FLOWER COLOR					BLOOMING SEASONS				SPECIAL USES						LIGHT			NIGHT TEMP.		
	Under 1 foot	1 to 2 feet	Over 2 feet	White-green	Yellow-orange	Pink-red	Blue-purple	Multicolor	Winter	Spring	Summer	Fall	Potted plant	Dish garden	Hanging basket	Rock garden	Ground cover	Specimen plant	Bright direct	Indirect or filtered	Artificial	45° to 55°	50° to 60°	60° to 70°
NEOPORTERIA CHILENSIS	●					●					●	●							●			●		
NEOPORTERIA NIDUS SENILIS	●		●			●					●	●	●						●			●		
NOTOCACTUS SCOPA (silver ball cactus)	●			●					●	●		●						●	●	●	●			
OBREGONIA DENEGRII (artichoke cactus)	●		●							●		●	●					●	●	●			●	
OPUNTIA BIGELOVII (teddy-bear cholla)			●	●	●					●		●			●		●	●	●	●				
OPUNTIA PAEDIOPHYLLA (paperspine cactus)	●			●	●					●		●			●			●	●	●				
PACHYPHYTUM COMPACTUM (thick plant)	●					●				●		●						●	●	●			●	
PARODIA ERYTHRANTHA	●					●			●	●		●	●						●	●		●		
PEDILANTHUS TITHYMALOIDES VARIEGATUS (variegated devil's backbone)		●	●								●				●			●	●	●				●
PERESKIA ACULEATA (lemon vine)		●	●	●	●					●	●							●	●			●		
PLEIOSPILOS BOLUSII (mimicry plant)	●			●				●	●	●		●	●					●			●	●		
PORTULACARIA AFRA VARIEGATA (rainbow bush)		●				●						●			●	●	●		●		●			
REBUTIA SENILIS (fire crown cactus)	●					●			●	●		●	●					●		●				
RHIPSALIS CRIBRATA		●	●						●					●				●	●	●				
RHIPSALIS PARADOXA (chain cactus)		●	●						●					●				●	●	●				
SANSEVIERIA TRIFASCIATA HAHNII (Hahn's sansevieria)	●												●					●	●	●				●
SCHLUMBERGERA BRIDGESII (Christmas cactus)	●	●				●	●		●				●		●				●				●	●
SCILLA VIOLACEA (silver squill)	●			●		●					●		●					●	●	●				●
SEDUM LINEARE VARIEGATUM (carpet sedum)	●			●					●	●		●	●	●	●	●		●					●	●
SEDUM RUBROTINCTUM (jelly beans)	●			●			●	●		●				●		●	●		●				●	●
SEDUM SPECTABILE (showy stonecrop)		●				●					●	●		●				●					●	●
SEDUM WEINBERGII (ghost plant)	●		●				●	●			●		●	●				●					●	●
SELENICEREUS GRANDIFLORUS (queen-of-the-night)		●	●								●					●		●	●					
SEMPERVIVUM ARACHNOIDEUM (cobweb houseleek)	●					●					●		●		●	●	●	●		●	●			
STAPELIA NOBILIS (noble-star-flower)	●				●		●			●		●						●	●	●				
THELOCACTUS BICOLOR (glory-of-Texas)	●					●	●				●		●		●			●	●	●		●		
TRICHOCEREUS SHAFERI		●		●							●		●					●	●	●	●	●		
WILCOXIA SCHMOLLII (lamb's-tail cactus)	●					●	●			●			●					●			●			
YUCCA FILAMENTOSA 'BRIGHT EDGE'		●	●								●							●	●			●		

*In the case of trailing plants, figures given apply to length of stems.

plants. Macmillan Publishing Co., 1975.

Higgins, Vera, Cactus Growing for Beginners, 4th ed. International Publications Service, 1971.

Higgins, Vera, Succulents in Cultivation. Blandford Press, London, 1960.

Jacobsen, Hermann, Lexicon of Succulent Plants. Blandford Press, London, 1974.

Lamb, Edgar, Colorful Cacti of the American Deserts. Macmillan Publishing Co., Inc., 1974.

Lamb, Edgar and Brian M., The Illustrated Reference on Cacti and Other Succulents. Blandford Press, London, 1955.

Lamb, Edgar and Brian, Pocket Encyclopedia of Cacti and Succulents in Color. Macmillan Publishing Co., Inc., 1970.

Lamb, Edgar and Brian, Popular Exotic Cacti in Color. Macmillan Publishing Co., Inc., 1976.

Marshall, W. Taylor, and Bock, Thor Methven, Cactaceae: With Illustrated keys of all tribes, sub-tribes and genera. Abbey Garden Press, 1941.

Martin, Margaret J., Chapman, P. R., and Auger, H. A., Cacti and Their Cultivation. Charles Scribner's Sons, 1971.

Merchants Publishing Co., Cacti and Succulents for Modern Living. 1976.

Mulligan, William C., Cacti and Succulents. Grosset & Dunlap, 1975.

Perry, Francis, Complete Guide to Plants and Flowers. Simon & Schuster, 1974.

Shewell-Cooper, W. E., and Rochford, T. C., Cacti as House Plants. Blandford Press, London, 1973.

Staff of the L. H. Bailey Hortorium, Cornell University, Hortus Third: A Dictionary of Plants Cultivated in the United States and Canada. Macmillan Publishing Co., 1976.

Storms, Ed, Growing the Mesembs. Tarrant Printing, 1976.

Subik, Rudolf, Decorative Cacti, A Guide to Succulent House Plants. The Hamlyn Publishing Group, Ltd., London, 1971.

Sunset Editors, Succulents and Cactus. Lane Publishing Co., 1975.

Van Ness, Martha, Cacti and Succulents Indoors and Outdoors. Van Nostrand Reinhold Co., 1971.

Wyman, Donald, Wyman's Gardening Encyclopedia. Macmillan Publishing Co., 1971.

Picture credits

The sources for the illustrations in this book are shown below. Credits from left to right are separated by semicolons, from top to bottom by dashes. All photographs by Enrico Ferorelli except: Cover: Entheos. 4: Philip Perl. 6: Plants from the collection of Dr. Gerald Barad. 9: Drawing by Kathy Rebeiz. 11 through 15: Plants from the collection of Dr. Gerald Barad. 17, 19: Drawings by Kathy Rebeiz. 20, 21: Drawings by Susan M. Johnston. 22: Drawing by Kathy Rebeiz. 25: Plant from the collection of Dr. Gerald Barad. 26: Entheos; plant from the collection of Dr. Gerald Barad. 27: Entheos; plants from the collection of Dr. Gerald Barad (2). 28: Plants from the collection of Dr. Gerald Barad. 29: Plants from the collection of Dr. Gerald Barad (2); Entheos. 30, 31: Plants from the collection of Dr. Gerald Barad. 35, 36, 41: Drawings by Kathy Rebeiz. 48, 49: Planting designed by Linda Trinkle Wolf. 52: Entheos. 55, 58: Drawings by Kathy Rebeiz. 63: Entheos. 64, 65: Terence Moore. 66, 67: F. A. Scherr. 68, 69: Louise Lippold. 70, 71, 72: Tom Tracy. 77: Entheos. 79, 80, 81: Drawings by Kathy Rebeiz. 83: Grafted by Dr. Gerald Barad. 84, 85, 86: Grafted by Frank Bowman, drawings by Susan M. Johnston. 87: Grafted by Dr. Gerald Barad (2); drawings by Susan M. Johnston. 88, 89: Grafted by Dr. Gerald Barad. 90: Illustration by Richard Crist. 92 through 149: Illustrations by artists listed in alphabetical order: Richard Crist, Rosemarie Francke, Susan M. Johnston, Mary Kellner, Charlotte Knox, Gwen Leighton, Trudy Nicholson, Eduardo Salgado, Ray Skibinski. 150: Map by Adolph E. Brotman.

Acknowledgments

The index for this book was prepared by Anita R. Beckerman. For their help in the preparation of this book, the editors wish to thank the following: Dr. Jules B. Aaron, Neponsit, N.Y.; Rupert Barnaby, New York Botanical Garden, The Bronx, N.Y.; Dr. Stephen L. Bosniak, Washington, D.C.; Frank Bowman, Brooklyn Botanic Garden, Brooklyn, N.Y.; Mrs. Roger Wilson Brett, Rancho Santa Fe, Calif.; Staff of the Brooklyn Botanic Garden, Brooklyn, N.Y.; Dr. James E. Canright, Department of Botany, Arizona State University, Tempe, Ariz.; Muriel Clarke, New York City; Michael de Santis, New York City; Earthworks of Park Slope, New York City; Elise Felton, The Philadelphia Cactus and Succulent Society, Philadelphia, Pa.; Karl Grieshaber, horticultural specialist, New York Botanical Garden, The Bronx, N.Y.; David B. Grigsby, Grigsby Cactus Gardens, Vista, Calif.; Wendy Hodgson, Department of Botany and Microbiology, Arizona State University, Tempe, Ariz.; Mr. Sidney Horenstein, American Museum of Natural History, New York City; Don Jones, East Creek Greenhouses, Holmdel, N.J.; Madelyn Lee, Vista, Calif.; Nancy H. Lewis, National Agricultural Library, Beltsville, Md.; Louise Lippold, Long Island, N.Y.; Rege and Wilma Malone, Leisure City, Fla.; Virginia F. Martin, President, Cactus Society of America, Arcadia, Calif.; John F. Mignone, East Meadow, N.Y.; Nabel's Nurseries Inc., White Plains, N.Y.; Staff of the New York Horticultural Society, New York City; Helen E. Payne, Oakhill Gardens, Dallas, Ore.; J. Liddon Pennock Jr., Meadowbrook Farm Greenhouse, Meadowbrook, Pa.; Lee M. Raden, Alpinflora, Phoenixville, Pa.; Sally Reath, Devon, Pa.; Helen Roubicek, Tucson, Ariz.; Mr. and Mrs. F. A. Scherr, Fla.; Dr. William Louis Stern, Division of Agricultural and Life Sciences, University of Maryland, College Park, Md.; Jean Tennant, New York City; Fred W. von Behren, Baltimore, Md.; Linda Trinkle Wolfe, horticultural interior designer, New York City.

Index

Numerals in italics indicate an illustration of the subject mentioned.

in desert garden, 60, 61; draining a dish garden, *41;* in outdoor garden, 54; after replanting, 35; requirements, 35
Watering mixed rock garden, 59
Wax agave. *See Echeveria*
Weeding, 61
Whisker cactus. *See Lophocereus*
White stonecrop. *See Sedum*

White-web ball cactus. *See Notocactus*
Wilcoxia, 148-149, *chart* 153; *poselgeri,30*
Window box planters, 57
Window plant. *See Haworthia*
Wrinkled pereskia, 9. *See also Pereskia*

Yellowing of plants, 59
Youth-and-old-age. *See Aichryson*

Yucca, 60, *149, chart* 153. *See also* Spanish bayonet; Spanish dagger

Zebra haworthia. *See Haworthia*
Zulu giant. *See Stapelia*
Zygocactus truncatus. See Schlumbergera

160